The Dog

First published 2021 by order of the Tate Trustees by Tate Publishing, a division of Tate Enterprises Ltd, Millbank, London SW1P 4RG

www.tate.org.uk/publishing

A catalogue record for this book is available from the British Library

ISBN 978-1-84976-739-2

Project Editor: Emma Poulter
Production: Roanne Marner
Picture Researcher: Emma O'Neill
Design: Joe Ewart
Colour reproduction by DL Imaging, London
Printed and bound in Italy by Printer Trento S.r.l.

MIX
Paper from responsible sources
FSC® C015829

The author
Emilia Will is an editor at Tate and freelance author. Interested in the intersection of fine art, popular culture, politics and folklore, she lives in South London where she spends her spare time growing things.

Cover:
Cedric Morris *Belle of Bloomsbury* 1948.
See p.81

Overleaf:
Joseph Bard *Photograph of Eileen Agar lying on a pebble beach at West Bay with her dog, Dandy* 1934. See p.54

The Dog

Emilia Will

TATE

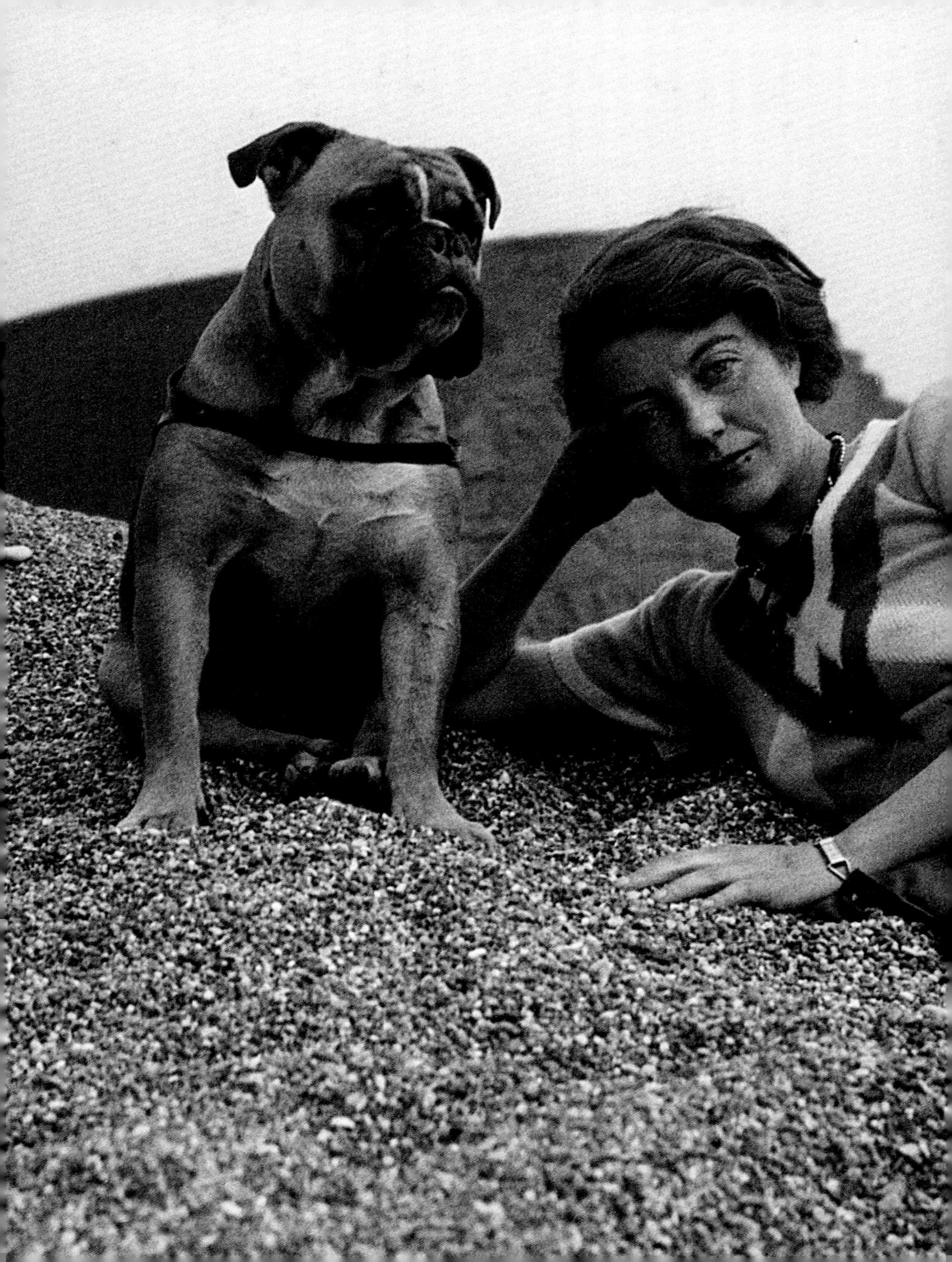

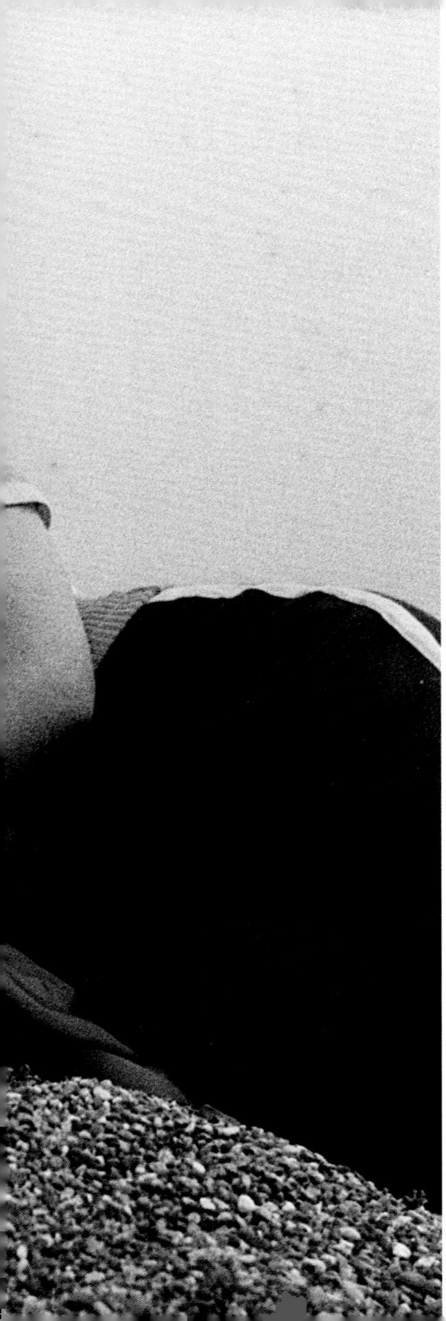

Every Dog has its Day

A small dog is trotting across the park, its paws padding the soft grass with each exultant step. All eyes are on the dog as it triumphantly saunters past amused bystanders, their hands scrambling for phones to take a photograph. Proud head held high and tail beating furiously, between its jaws is the most prized of possessions, the most coveted *objet d'art*: the humble stick.

Rewind over 8,000 years, and in Saudi Arabia, another dog is utterly absorbed in chewing a bone while its prehistoric human is diligently etching away into the cliffside. Slowly, a scene unfolds, dynamic and gripping: a figure is threading an arrow, seconds away from taking aim, while all around leap angular dogs, some leashed to the figure, some depicted with identifying markings, all desperate for the hunt.

Señor Xolotl has just woken up from his nap in Coyoacán, Mexico. He yawns and stretches his hairless body out on the sun-baked terrace as his mistress puts away her paintbrushes. It is 1945 and Frida Kahlo has just finished painting him into her self-portrait. With his ancient roots in Mesoamerican civilisations, Señor Xolotl, who is named after the Aztec dog-headed god of lightning and death, is her most beloved pet and proud nationalist emblem.

Fast-forward twenty years and Keith Arnatt has just taken his last shot in a series of photographs of dogs and their owners in his home town of Tintern, Monmouthshire. As he packs away his camera and returns home, the night draws in, and high above him, in the sloe-black sky, twinkles the gargantuan dog constellation of Canis Major, identified by Ptolemy in the second century.

In Buckingham Palace Her Majesty the Queen is enjoying a cup of tea while her corgis snuffle for crumbs at her feet. The paintings on the walls around her capture her family's legacy, and the pedigree of generations of royal dogs – from Edwin Landseer's portrait of Queen Victoria's (1819–1901) spaniel Dash, to Van Dyck's painting of King Charles I's (1600–49) children and their mastiff. Just around the corner is the gift shop, resplendent with toy corgis, corgi-decorated socks and British bulldog charms.

Whether it's Argos, the devoted dog of classical Greek Odysseus, Anubis the ancient Egyptian god of the underworld, Dorothy's Toto or the heroic Lassie, canines have been immortalised in visual culture and literature for thousands of years. This selection of artworks showcases the endeavours of artists in over three centuries of Western art to capture the harmonious and very special relationship between dogs and humans, uncovering images of companionship, cooperation and above all the steadfast love we humans have for our closest animal friend.

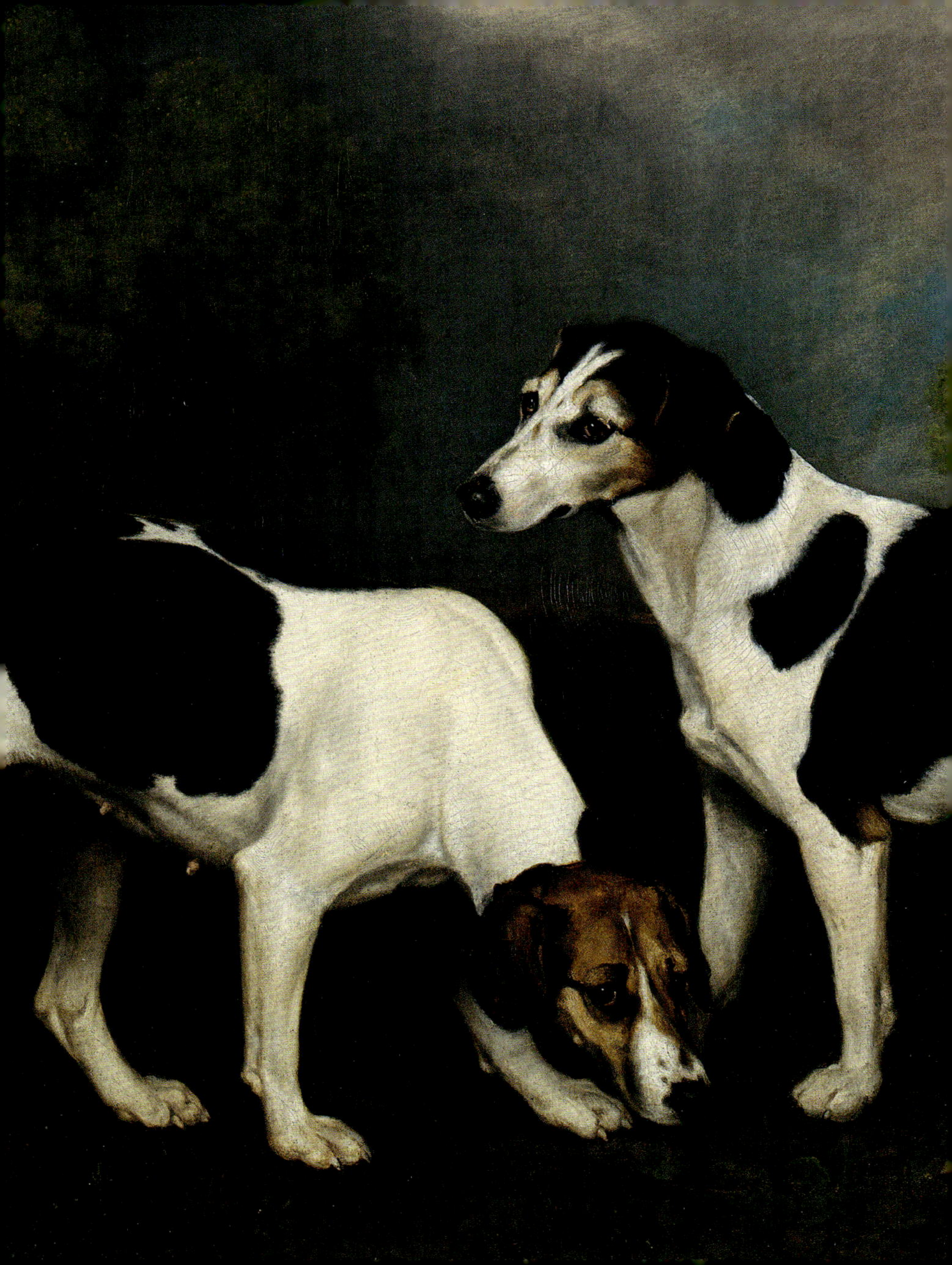

Hounds of the Hunt

Depictions of hounds have long been used to signify status in Europe, where wealth and nobility were conflated with a divine right to rule. In medieval England, rigid Forest Laws were imposed, privatising large swathes of the country and changing hunting from a necessity to the sport of the wealthy. Hunting on the king's land without permission was poaching, and punishable, and these restrictions led to larger land rights issues in the UK, including the enclosure of common lands some five hundred years later. Restricted access also applied to dogs, and the barbaric practice of 'lawing' (to make lawful) was carried out by maiming dogs belonging to those living on or near the 'forest' lands. The plight of the poacher is part of a larger counter-culture in the UK, with figures such as Robin Hood becoming national heroes. Although poachers and their dogs rarely feature in classical hunting paintings, which would have been commissioned by wealthy landowners, they are immortalised in folk songs such as 'Thorneymoor Woods', which commemorates the poachers operating in the enclosed 'forest' land of Sherwood.

In essence the Norman laws started the divisive nature of hunting today. Historical representations of hunting dogs were almost always used to represent the owner's own noble nature, and demonstrated their wealth, social standing and dominance.

GEORGE STUBBS ***A Couple of Foxhounds*** 1792
(detail, see p.16)

PETER TILLEMANS

Foxhunting in Wooded Country c.1720–30

Flemish painter Tillemans was one of the first artists to produce hunting paintings in Britain, and would lead a great tradition in the subject. Idealised, Italianate rural settings in a classical style belie the reality of country life and the divisions within society. Beagles, bloodhounds, greyhounds and foxhounds were the elite dogs in boar-, deer-, hare- and foxhunting while smaller terriers or mixed breeds, such as lurchers, were generally used by the working class to poach food and catch vermin.

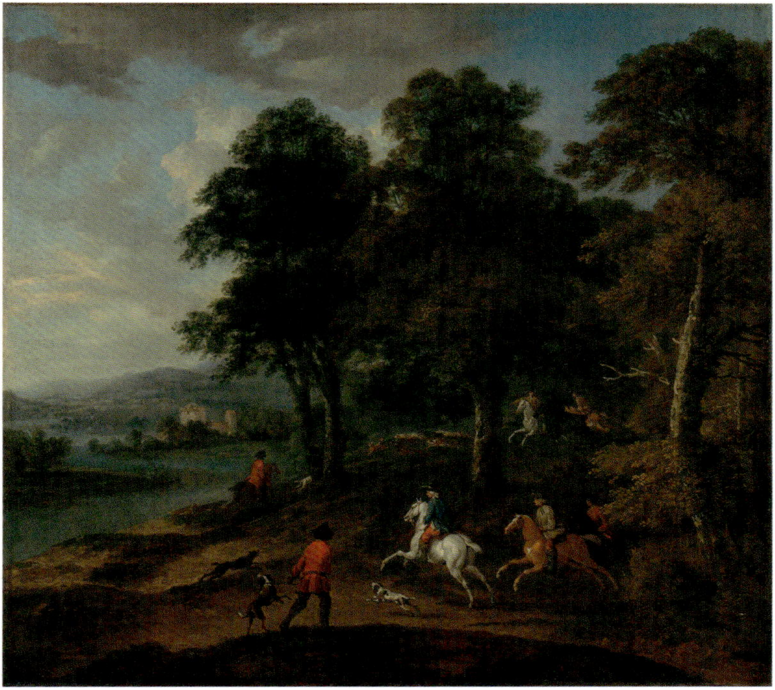

ATTRIBUTED TO JAMES SEYMOUR

Pointer Bitch c.1740

Attributed to James 'Jimmy' Seymour, an avid lover of all things equestrian, who bankrupted his own father through living 'gay high and loosely', this painting is likely a portrait commission of a most precious hound. Her owner is unknown but a thistle in the corner indicates possible Scottish connections. The dog's pose and odd perspective create an illusion that it is superimposed onto the background and aligns it with a 'naïve' style. The pointer takes its name from the stance it adopts when it detects the scent of game, also known as the quarry.

JOHN NOST SARTORIUS

The Earl of Darlington Fox-Hunting with the Raby Pack: Going to Cover 1805

William Harry Vane, the 3rd Earl of Darlington is pictured here in black hat and riding breeches, at the 'chase'. Passionate about foxhunting, he kept hounds at his home, Raby Castle, for nearly fifty years, hunted six days a week and religiously kept a diary for each hunting season. Here eager foxhounds leap across the hills of Teesdale. Sartorius flatters them here; each is shown in profile, their lean bodies seen at the best possible angle, demonstrating their agility and skill, with noses pointing towards the quarry.

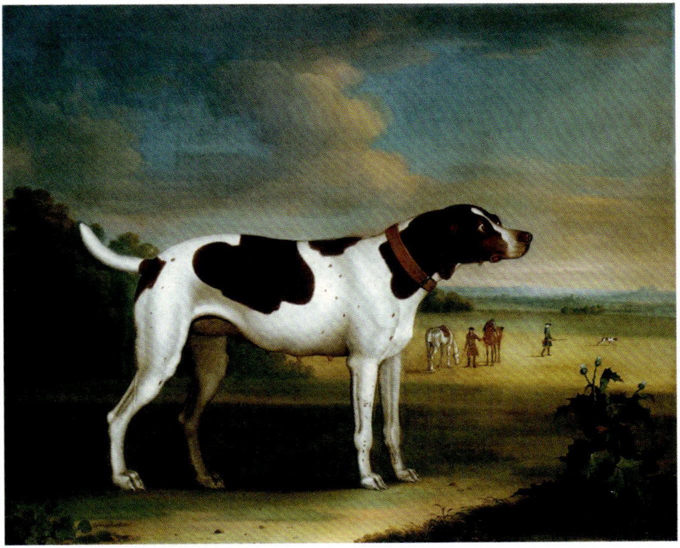

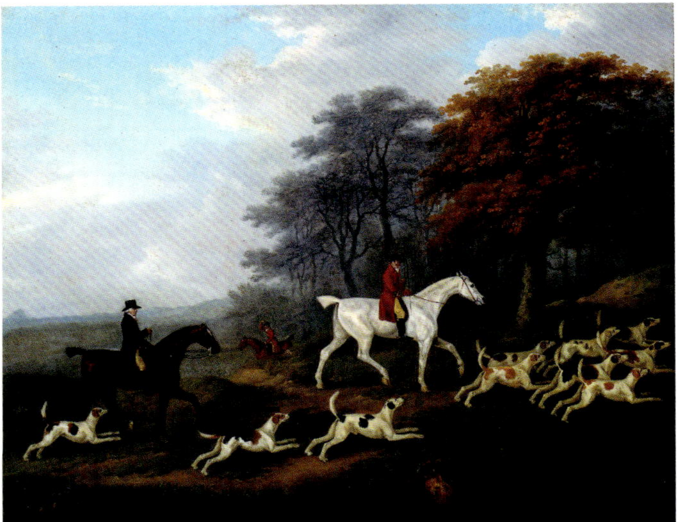

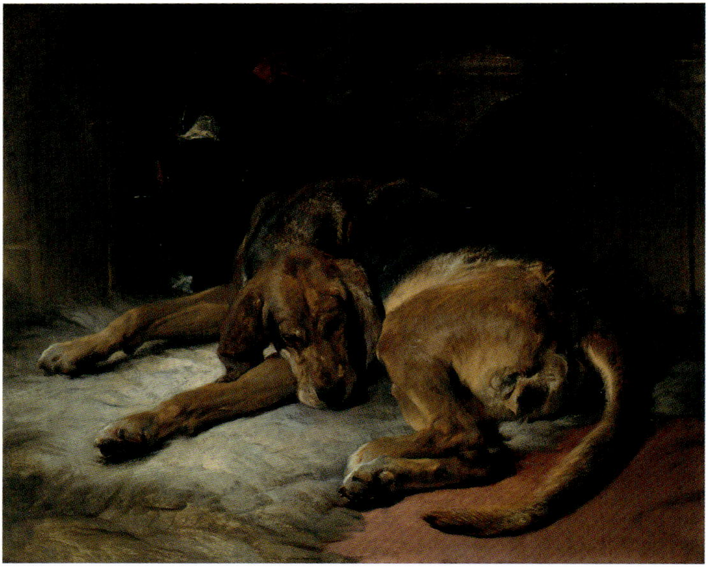

EDWIN HENRY LANDSEER

Sleeping Bloodhound exhibited 1835

This bloodhound has flopped down, utterly exhausted by the activities of the day. Placed in an imagined medieval setting, with a knight's helmet in the shadows, Landseer's painted dog references the bloodhound's cultural origins. First bred by medieval French monks to hunt boar or deer, these large dogs are now loved for their sweet and gentle natures, although they still have a place with police forces and search and rescue missions thanks to their incredibly powerful sense of smell.

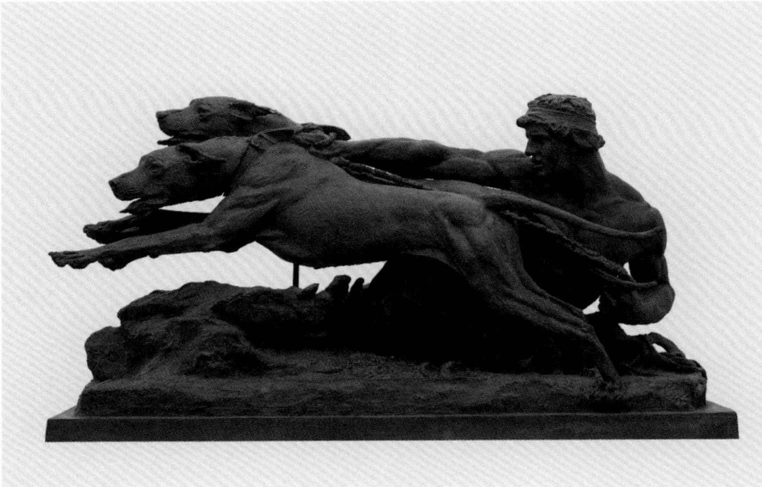

HARRY BATES

Hounds in Leash 1888–9

These Great Danes are power and drama embodied. Straining at their leashes, desperate for the hunt and depicted with an intensity of muscle, the dogs in this impressive plaster sculpture are full of energy and movement. The Earl of Wemyss and March commissioned a twin to this piece in bronze to be placed outside his neoclassical country house in East Lothian. The classical style suits the grand Italianate building, with Michelangelo's god-like athletic bodies. Bates studied live dog models and the work is said to have been delayed after one of the dogs was affected by paralysis during the sittings, and died.

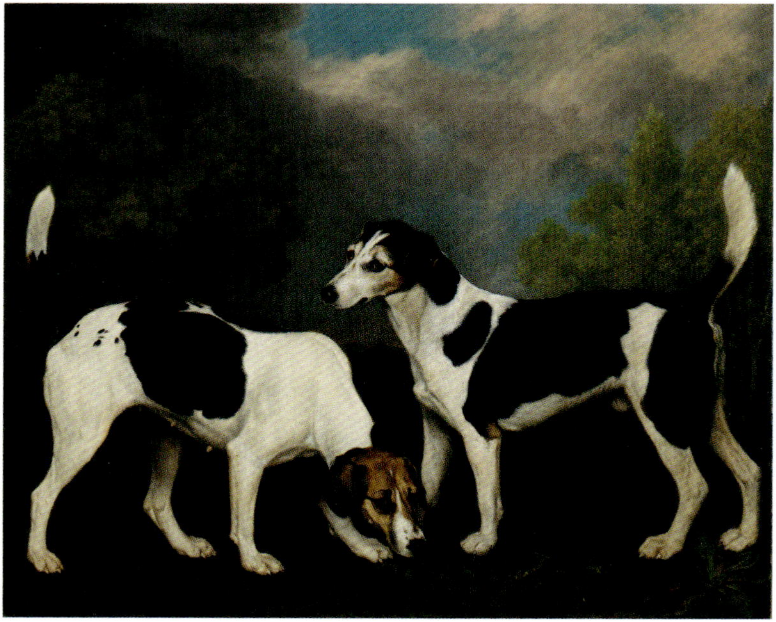

GEORGE STUBBS

A Couple of Foxhounds 1792

Although the title suggests this sweet pair of dogs are foxhounds, their actual breed is uncertain, and it has been suggested that they are harriers, dogs traditionally used to sniff out hares for hunting. Here the female of the two is demonstrating her prowess in smelling, with her nose to the ground. Both their eyes remain on us, obedient and looking for praise. This painting, commissioned by hound breeder the Reverend Thomas Vyner of Lincolnshire, would have served as both an advert for his exceptional breeding skills but also as a memento of his favourite dogs.

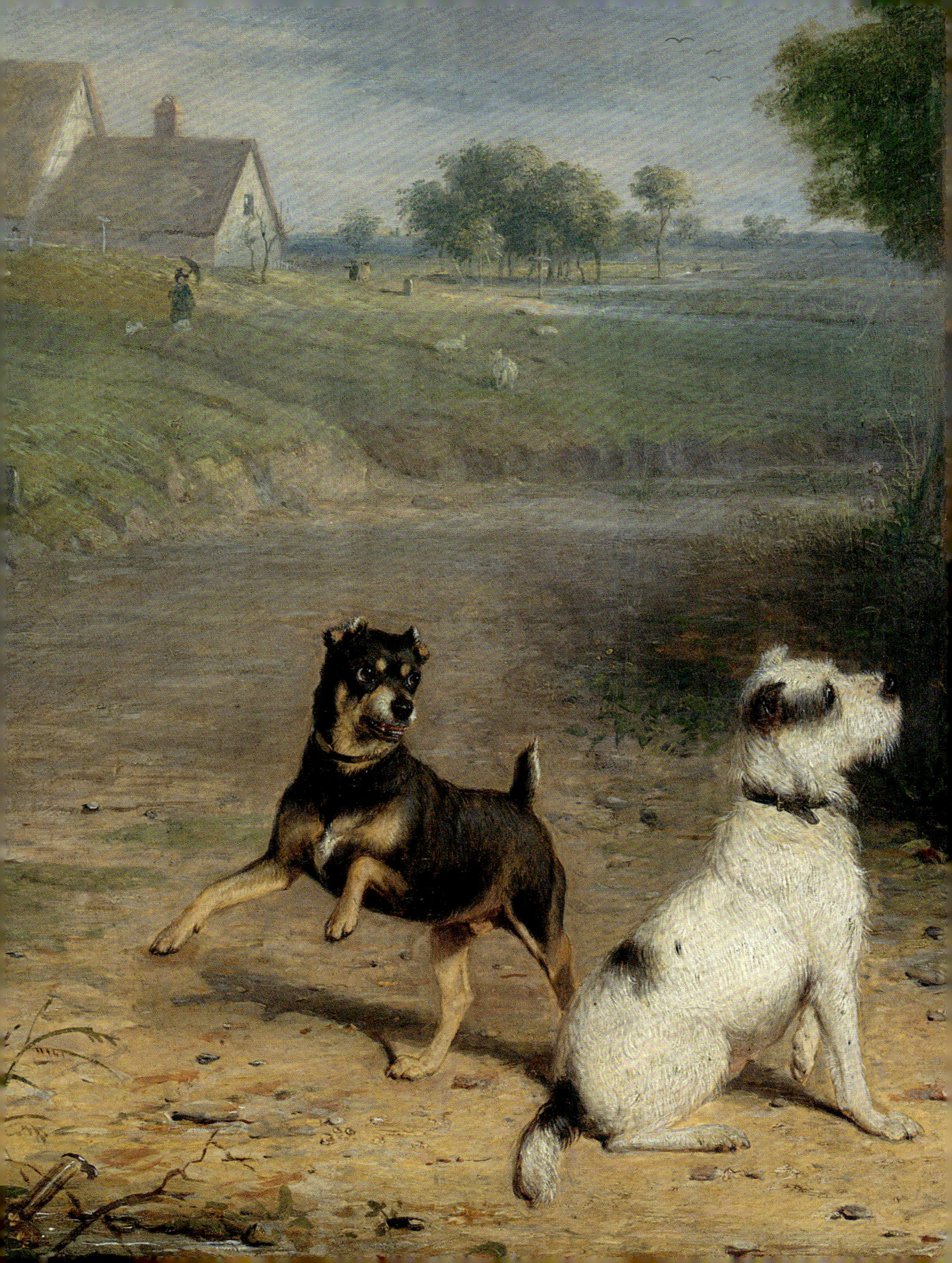

Working Like a Dog

We've all witnessed the tenacity of a dog hard at work – whether it's a collie rounding up sheep, a golden retriever guiding its human across a busy station or huskies pulling sledges. Dedication to their tasks is second to none and, thanks to their loyal nature and willingness to please, they will perform a great many roles for us without complaint, for better or worse. The ancient Greek breed of mastiffs (*molossus*) were utilised by the Romans as battle dogs and guards; 'beware of the dog' mosaics have been found in Pompeii, Italy. Carriage or coach dogs protected horse-drawn carriages, with Dalmatians becoming a favourite in the early nineteenth century, serving at fire stations by clearing the streets ahead of engines. Galleries in the 1930s employed trained dogs to protect artworks (p.26) and dogs patrolled at the Louvre, Paris, Boston Museum of Fine Arts, the Fogg Museum in Cambridge, Massachusetts, and the Museum of Modern Art, New York (MoMA). In warfare, dogs throughout history have bravely obeyed our commands (p.30) – as sentries, runners, messengers or by ridding soldiers of rats in the trenches.

It is no surprise that the phrase 'working like a dog' endures in our vocabulary, and images of them hard at work frequently appear in visual art.

THOMAS WOODWARD ***The Rat Catcher and his Dogs*** exhibited 1824 (detail, see p.23)

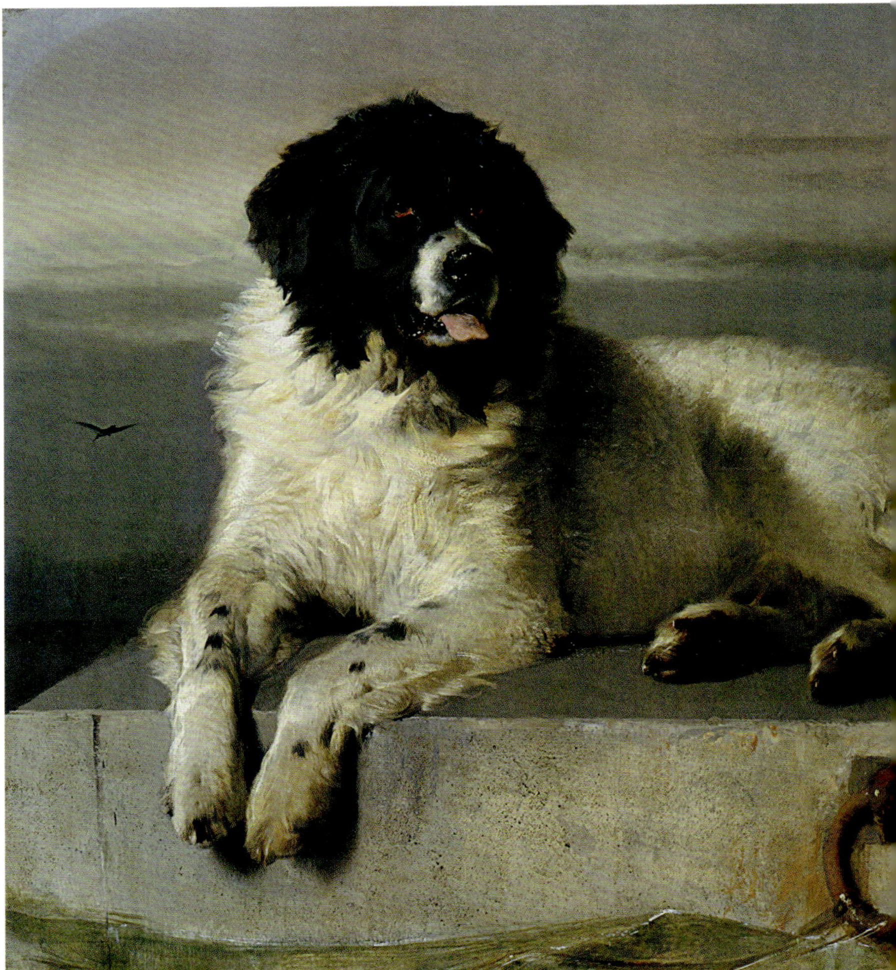

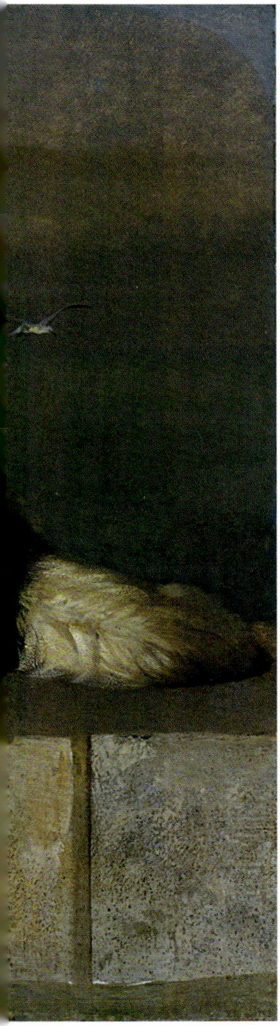

EDWIN HENRY LANDSEER

A Distinguished Member of the Humane Society
exhibited 1838

Legend tells that Bob, a noble Newfoundland, almost drowned in a shipwreck off the coast of England, and soon after started work as a lifeguard on the banks of the River Thames, where he saved a total of twenty-three people. 'Newfies' are known for their excellent swimming abilities thanks to their webbed paws and thick coat, protecting them from the cold. As Bob was busy saving lives when Landseer painted this, he wasn't able to sit for the portrait, and so Paul Pry, another dog, stood in for him. It seems Bob (Paul) had an inescapable connection with water, for this painting was subject to damage in the infamous floods at Tate Britain in 1928, and it took almost eighty years for him to be restored to his former glory. The piebald variety of Newfoundland was made so popular by Landseer that there is now a strand of the breed named in honour of him.

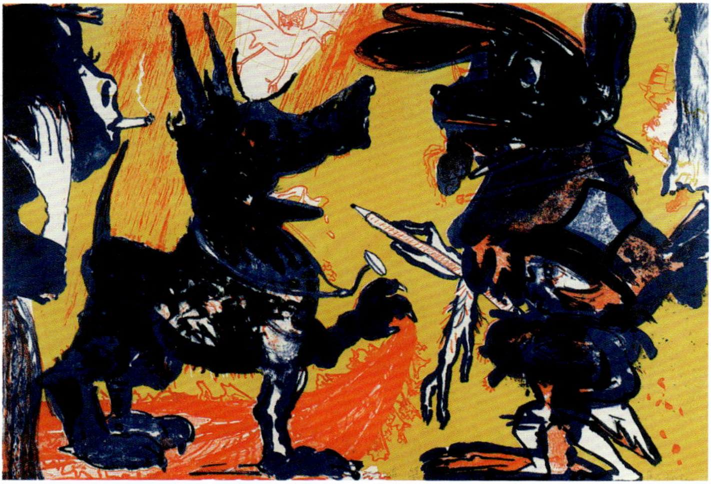

PAULA REGO

Doctor Dog 1982

Doctor Dog might have seemed like a surreal, perhaps even nightmarish, scene when it was first made forty years ago, with the doctor's drooling mouth and bloody sky behind. Although the violence in this lithograph hasn't diminished, a contemporary viewer might recognise the sense in having a canine carer to alleviate mental health issues. It marks the beginning of Rego's long relationship with painting dogs, figurative fidos that represented her unwell husband or sometimes women, culminating with the infamous *Dog Woman* 1994, a feral and powerful image of a woman on all fours barking.

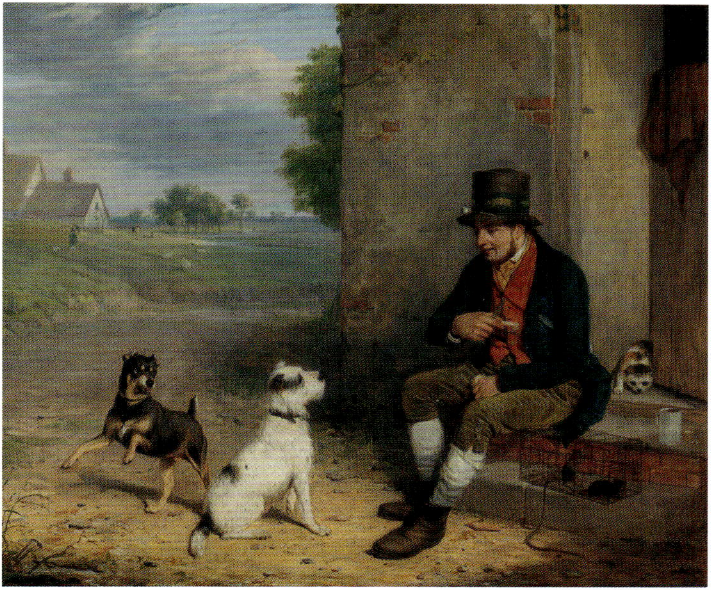

THOMAS WOODWARD

The Rat Catcher and his Dogs exhibited 1824

Two 'ratters' – possibly a Jack Russell and a Manchester terrier – await a bone about to be tossed by their boss, the village rat catcher, a profession which still continues to this day. The ribbon or band around this working man's hat identifies him, in case the cage of rats wasn't obvious enough. Beside his day job, it is quite possible that this relatively well-dressed man supplemented his salary with the lucrative blood sport of rat-baiting.

SIDNEY NOLAN

Landscape – Miner with Dog 1973

Nolan is most famous for his bleak, raw landscapes of the Australian bush and its infamous outlaw, Ned Kelly. Ned, a restless silhouette in his black box of a helmet, repeatedly appears in Nolan's works. Here, another figure is pictured in a helmet, a necessary protection for such an occupation as mining. Dogs are increasingly utilised by mining companies to sniff out metal ores, although it is unclear where exactly this dog is working. The fiery smudge of the miner's face blends into the scorched earth behind him, while his trusty companion sits upright and alert, ready for work.

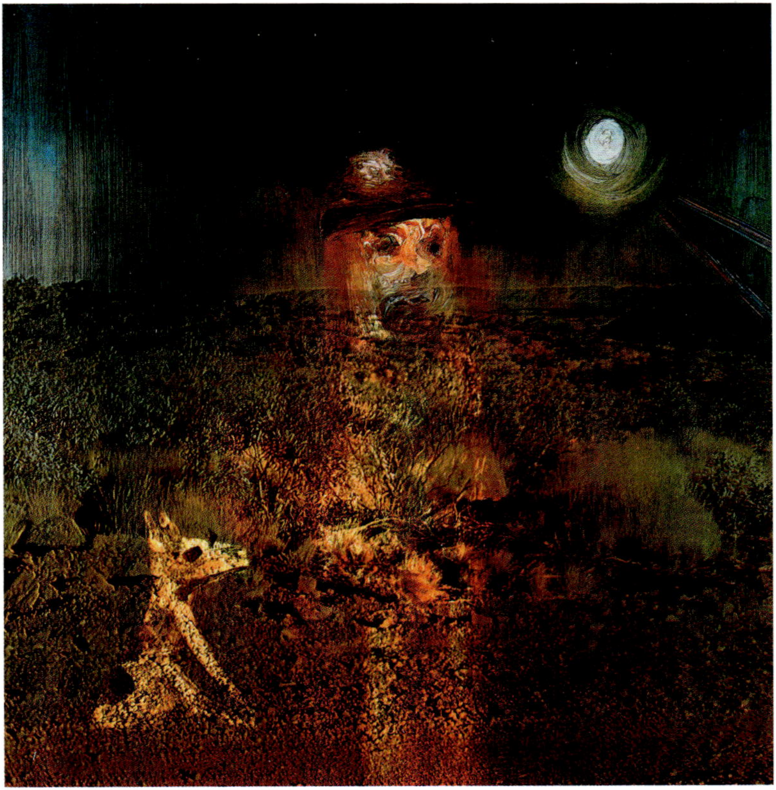

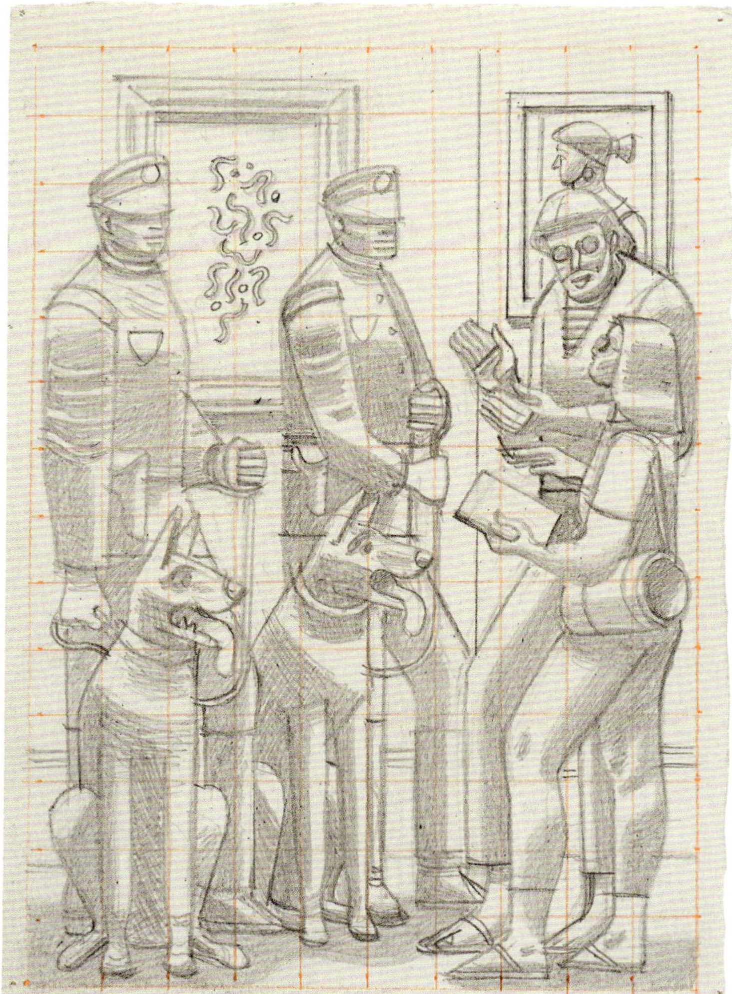

WILLIAM ROBERTS

Study for 'Guarding the Masterpiece' c.1964

Despite their colleagues' aggressive, militaristic uniforms, these tubular mutts look far from ferocious. Great lolloping tongues hang from their mouths as two gallery visitors talk fervently about the artwork the dogs guard. Roberts was known for his fastidious use of a grid, and in this study his pen marks can be seen dividing and ordering the page. In the 1930s, when museum guard dogs were popular, MoMA's dog Don was advertised as being so vicious he could bite through a plank of wood. However, after just a month his gentle nature shone through, and he had to be retrained because he was too friendly with the museum's visitors.

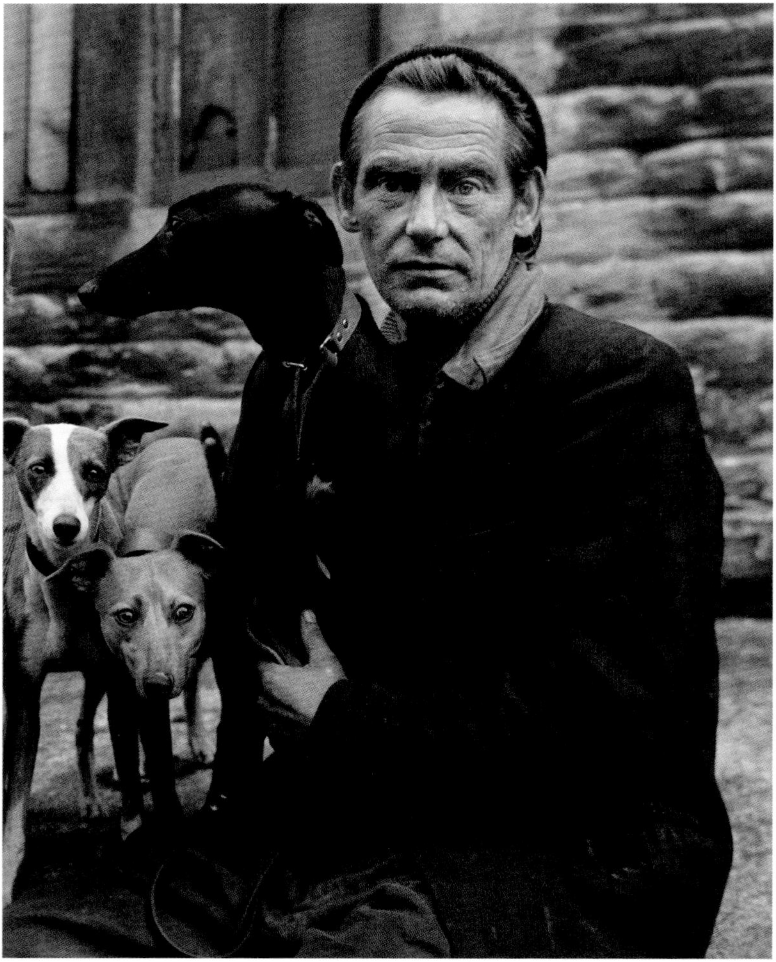

CHRIS KILLIP

Whippet Fancier 1973, printed 2012–13

This is one of six black-and-white photographs from the series *Huddersfield, Yorkshire* 1973–4. Killip's practice focussed on building relationships with the people (and animals) in the communities he photographed. Here both man and dogs seem familiar with their photographer; the whippets are keenly leaning in to say hello while one is so unfazed by the lens he casually turns away, offering his elegant profile. Fanciers bred and dealt in dogs for a living, but this man gently holds onto his companion, whose shoulder affectionately reclines on his chest in return. Perhaps this one will stay.

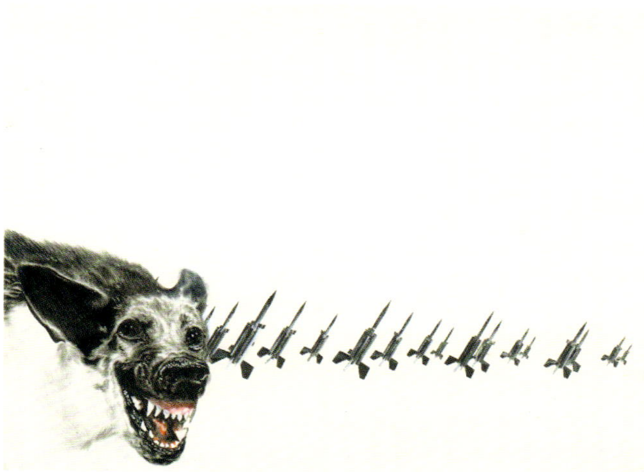

COLIN SELF

Guard Dog on a Missile Base, No. 1 1965

The weaponisation of dogs has a long and troubling history. Easily trained and loyal to a fault, canines can carry out difficult tasks such as locating explosives, as well as performing intimidation tactics. During the 1960s Self's work was concerned with Cold War politics and nuclear war. This work was inspired after he spent a weekend near a nuclear missile base in Norfolk, England, where they stored Bristol Bloodhound missiles. The haunting name of this weapon of mass destruction alludes to the homing abilities of bloodhounds. In a letter, Self wrote, 'By night the howling of guard dogs chilled the air and imagination. Animal and technological threat were united in one fearful ground.'

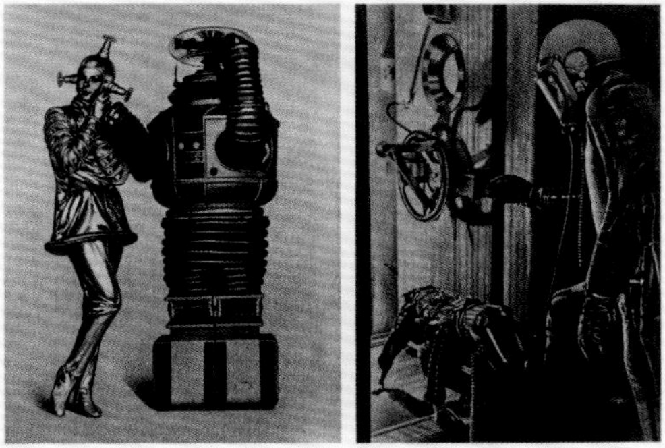

EDUARDO PAOLOZZI

H. Left: Television Series 'Lost in Space': Robot as in 'Forbidden Planet'. Right: Soviet Dog and Man Exit from Space Chamber 1971

Scottish pioneer of pop art, Paolozzi employed a professional retoucher to edit these photographic images and then photoetch them, as they were often from poor-quality newspapers. As a result the etchings look more like paintings, giving an uncanny quality. In this one a patient space dog waddles towards an idealised astronaut, its little legs akimbo in the clunky suit. It looks like the work of science fiction, but dogs were a vital part of the 1950s space race, with Soviet space dog Laika being the first ever animal to orbit the Earth's giddy stratospheres.

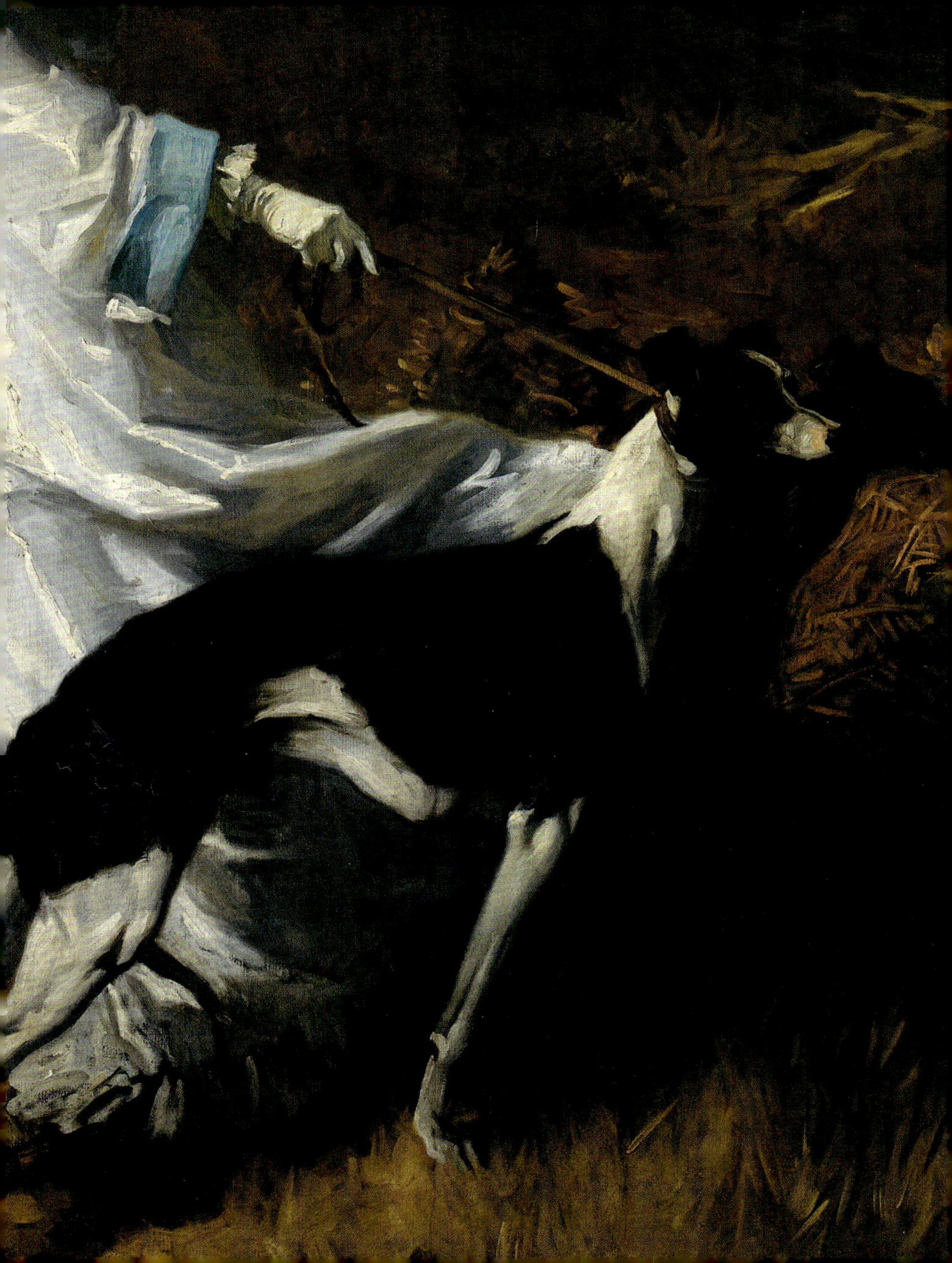

Mythical Mutts

Our relationship with dogs is written into the stars, and our interpretation of the universe tells the story of our bond with them. The dog occupies the eleventh position in the Chinese zodiac, and those that are born under it are said to be faithful and honest. Sirius, the brightest star in the sky, makes up part of the constellation of Canis Major, the great dog Laelaps in an eternal chase across the galaxy.

Legends of dogs feature in most cultures around the world and are woven into stories, from religious narratives to local folklore. Art and literature are vehicles for telling these stories and ensuring their longevity. Saint Roch, the Christian patron saint of dogs, is depicted in medieval paintings and sculptures with an altruistic pup that licked his plague sores, restoring him to health. The loyalty of dogs is celebrated in epic poems and fables: Argos, the loving hound of Odysseus, is immortalised in Homer's *Odyssey*, and through myths such as that of tragic Welsh hero Gelert, a dog who saved his lord's baby from a wolf is remembered.

Conversely, canines can appear in our nightmares and imaginations as spectral dogs, werewolves, hellhounds and guardians to the underworld. In Oaxaca, Mexico, black dogs are believed to help the deceased cross rivers and seas to the land of the dead, while Bhairava, the fierce form of the Hindu deity of destruction, is recognised in visual culture by his mount – a dog or Shvan who accompanies him everywhere.

CHARLES WELLINGTON FURSE *Diana of the Uplands* 1903–4
(detail, see p.36)

PAUL McCARTHY

Dog 2000

The two faces of this sitter may allude to Cerberus, the ancient Greek three-headed hellhound of the underworld, and yet the eyes are too gentle and the fluffy tufts on its chest too soft. Multiple images have been superimposed, marking the passage of time as the dog turns and lifts its head to bark. McCarthy took 120 Polaroids in total of his German shepherd as its health declined. When it eventually passed away, it became immortalised in this image; a true mythical mutt.

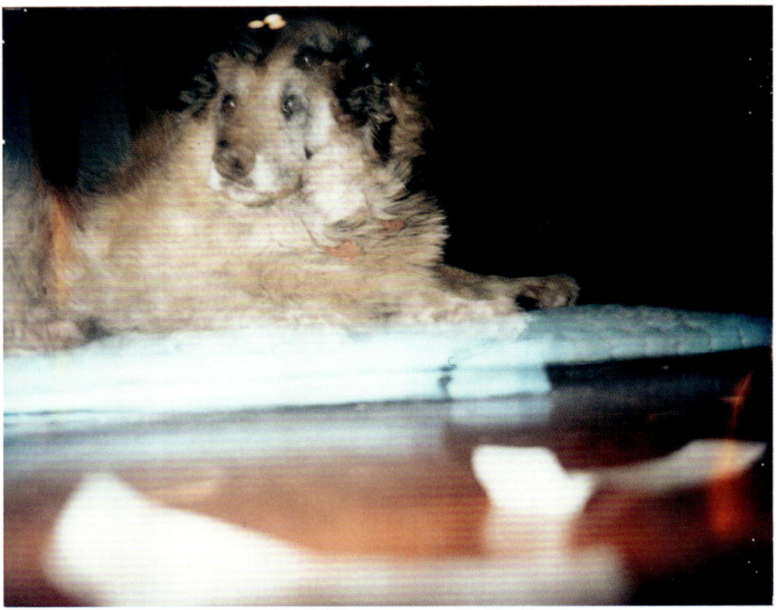

EDWIN HENRY LANDSEER

Alexander and Diogenes 1848

Each dog here has its own symbolic meaning in an ancient philosophical allegory. The proud white bulldog is Alexander the Great; the scruffy mutt in the shadows is the Cynic philosopher, Diogenes. Diogenes was often associated with dogs, having lived a life stripped of material pleasures, supposedly in an old wine cask, like a stray dog in the street. The guard dogs of the king stand vigilant in the background, while puppy punters in their finery, with ribbons, collars and glossy coats, all draw a stark comparison to the rough but happy life of the philosopher.

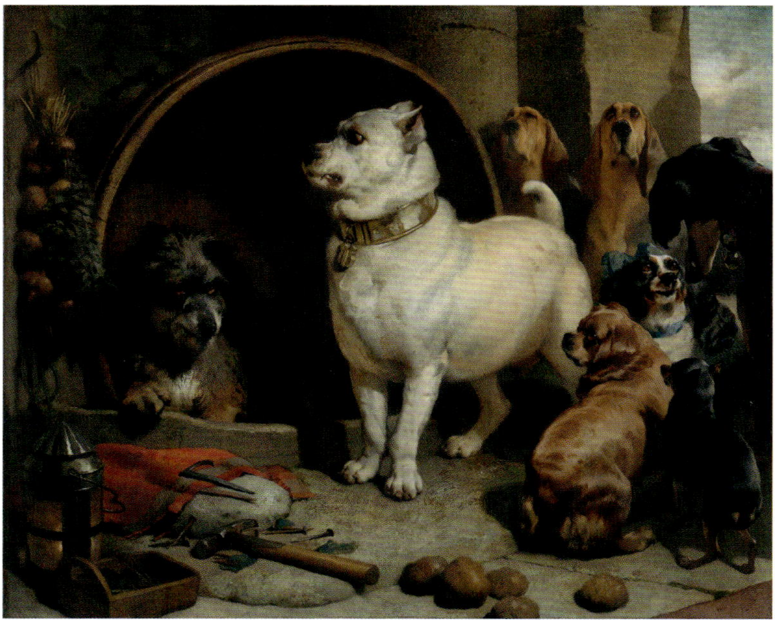

CHARLES WELLINGTON FURSE

Diana of the Uplands 1903–4

Two greyhounds were hired for this action shot. One was white and one was black, but Furse had wanted to have a piebald mutt so combined the two on the canvas to create the desired effect. The figure is the artist's wife, Katherine Furse, posing as Diana, the Roman goddess of the hunt, who is typically depicted with her hunting hounds. Her stepmother-in-law Gertrude is out of shot, valiantly working the bellows to create the wind effect in her billowing skirts.

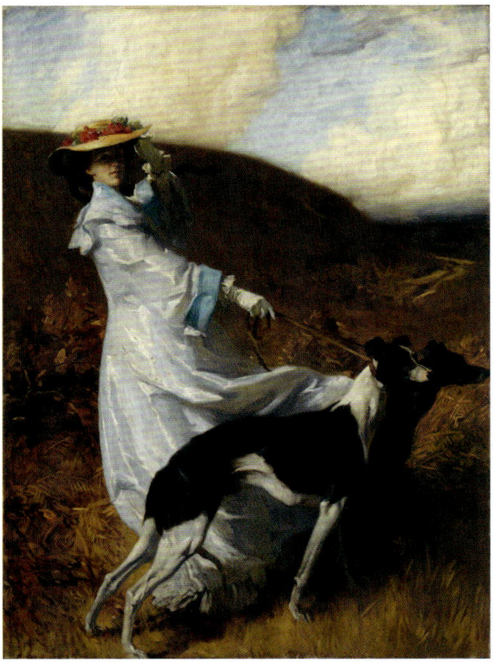

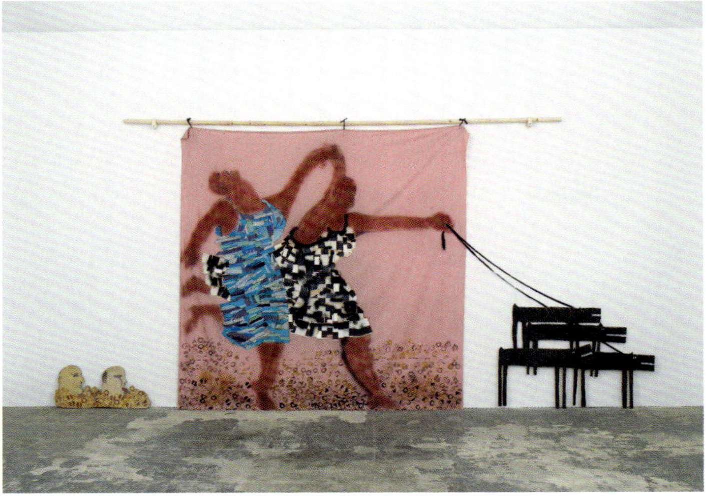

LUBAINA HIMID

Freedom and Change 1984

Painted on a pink bedsheet, two women leap across a beach, a pack of dogs lead them swiftly onwards. In their wake, two men buried up to their necks in sand literally eat their dust. Comparisons can be drawn to the huntress Diana, but here is reference to a different goddess: Venus, the goddess of love. Venus symbol earrings suggest that perhaps these women are romantically linked. In reinterpreting Picasso's *Two Women Running on the Beach (The Race)* 1922, Himid allows these women to reclaim their space in history as Black women, but in particular as Black lesbians, moving purposefully and passionately.

JACOB HUYSMANS

Portrait of a Lady, as Diana c.1674

Three greyhounds hide within the weightless fabrics and nebulous shadows of this painting by Flemish artist Huysmans. One nose can be seen protruding from the edge of the canvas on the right; one dog in the centre is the recipient of a celestial steadying hand on his neck, and the other dog lurks in the gloaming on the left. They are the actors in this performance of pageantry, playing the part of the goddess's hunting hounds. Huysmans's figurative portrait is typical of the flamboyant Baroque courtly style. This particular *masque*, or play, may have taken place in the court of King Charles II (1630–85) at Whitehall, London.

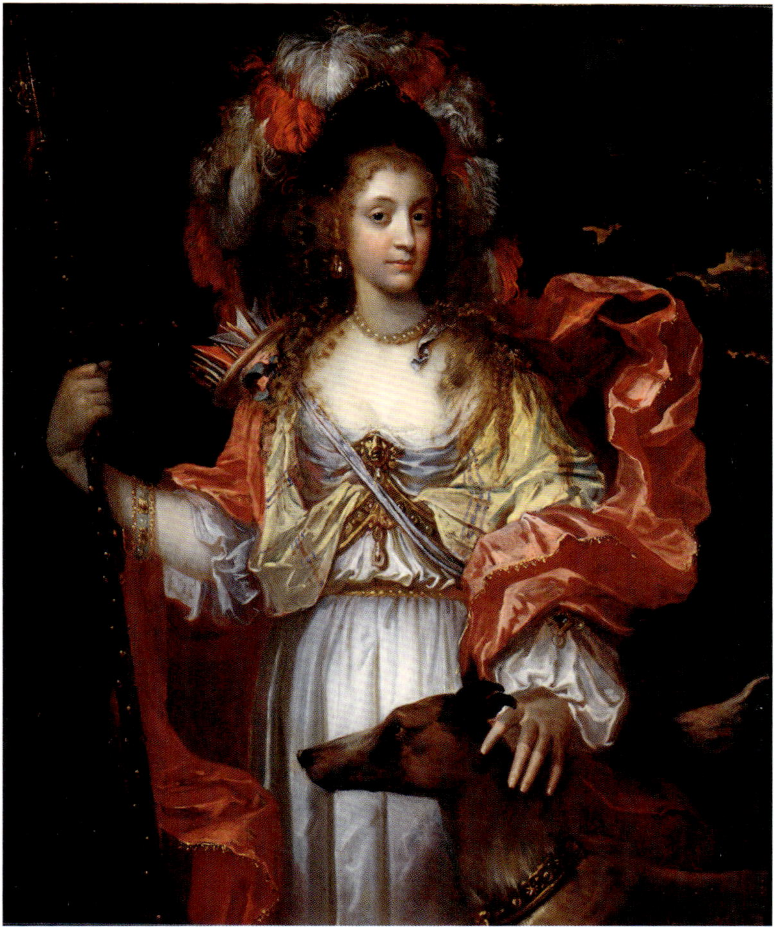

JOHN MURPHY

Investigations of a Dog (Pictor) 1984–96

Murphy named this work after a text written by Franz Kafka (1883–1924) in which a dog ruminates over his own existence and the meaning of life: 'For what is there apart from dogs? To whom else can one appeal in an otherwise empty world? All science, the totality of all questions and all answers, lies with us dogs.' The constellation under which this dog prowls is Pictor, otherwise known as the easel, which was used to symbolise artists trying to make sense of the world. Here artist and dog are one, both in search of cosmic comprehension.

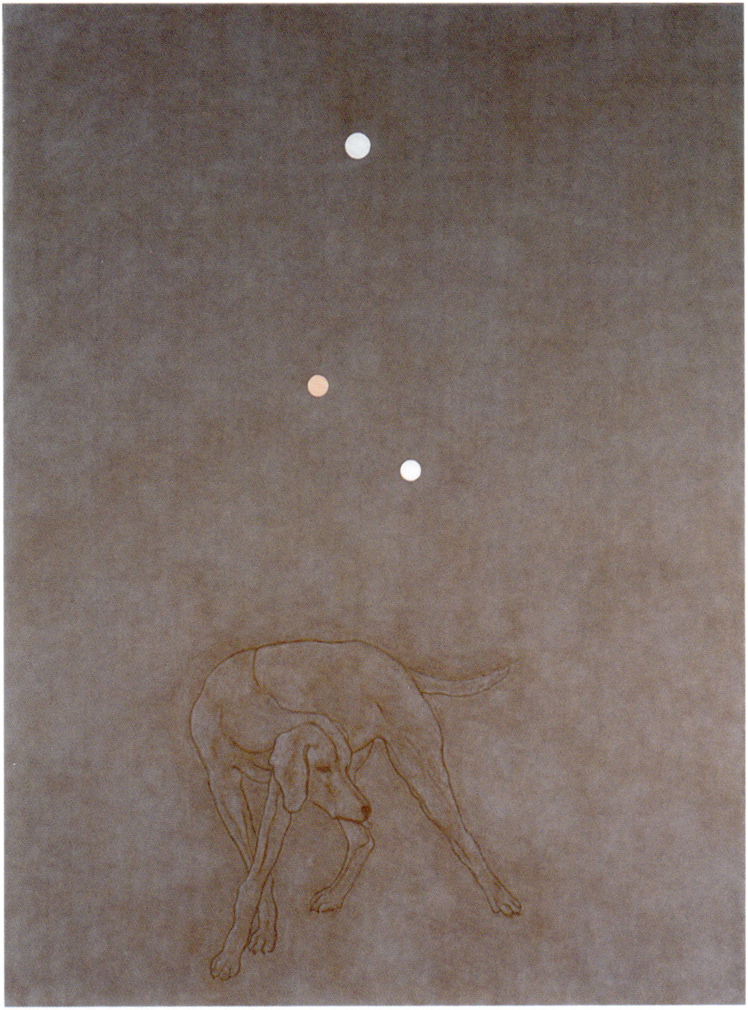

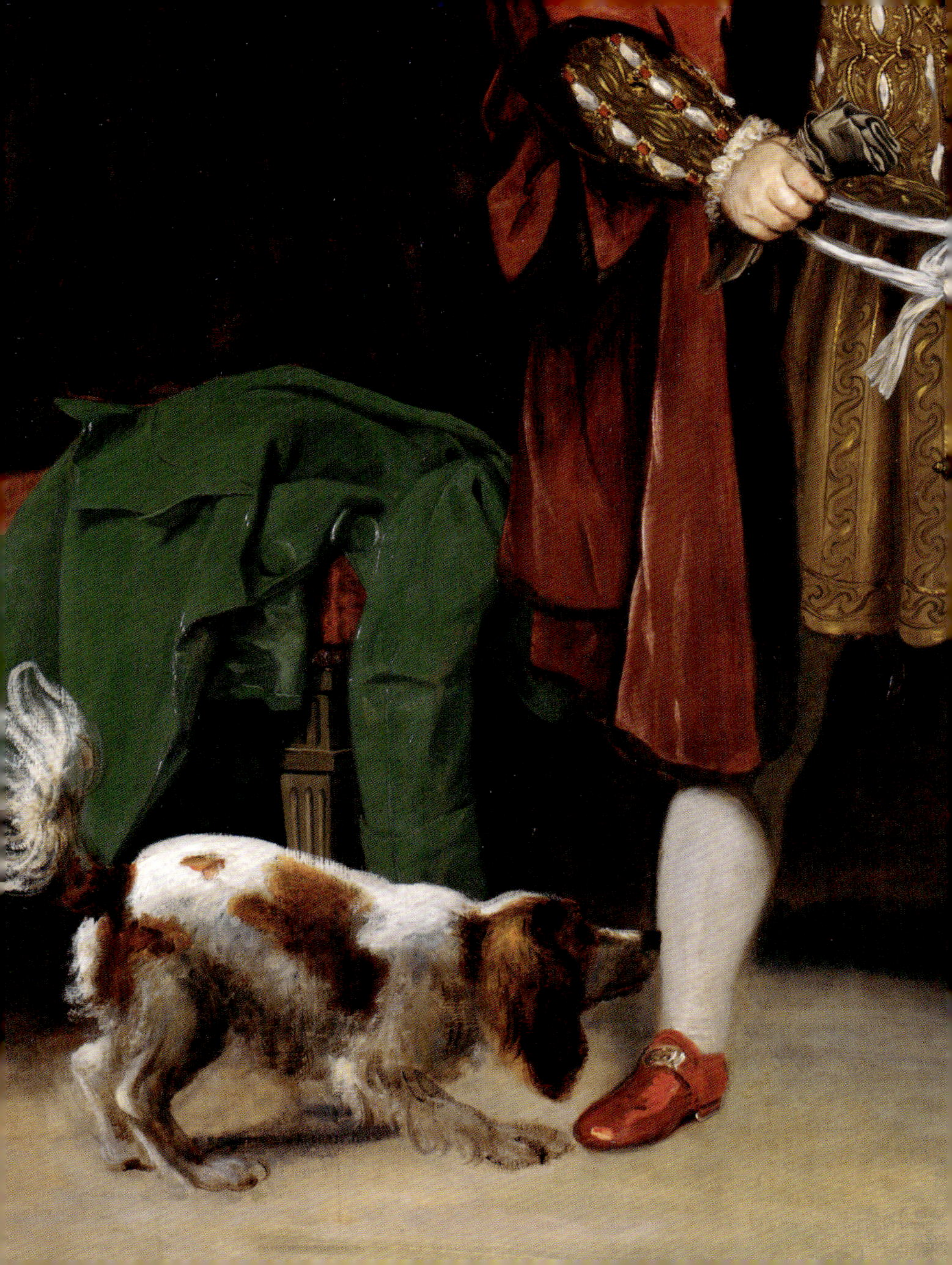

Princely Pups

Dogs and the aristocracy have a long history. Dogs bound along the Bayeux Tapestry, proclaiming the nobility and superiority of the Norman invaders. These were likely greyhounds or possibly Talbots, a type of white medieval hound that features in illuminated manuscripts and heraldic coats of arms. Sculptures of hounds stand sentinel over sweeping drives to stately homes (see p.15).

Certain breeds have enjoyed the patronage of wealthy dynasties, from dainty Pekingese at the Chinese Imperial court, to immense mastiffs and flamboyant spaniels, which Anthony van Dyck (1599–1641) painted in all their pomp alongside the Stuart monarchy.

Miniature or 'toy' dogs were favoured by gentlewomen at court, appearing in paintings as symbols of fidelity, but they were also confidants in troublesome times. Mary, Queen of Scots (1542–87) had many faithful dogs, and it is said one was so loyal that it refused to leave her body after she was beheaded, hiding in her skirts. Dogs have long been the silent companions of kings and queens, never disclosing secrets and always obediently heeling. On the epitaph of her beloved dog, Dash, Queen Victoria (1819–1901) had inscribed '... His attachment was without selfishness, His playfulness without malice, His fidelity without deceit. Reader, if you would live beloved and die regretted, profit by the example of Dash'.

JOSHUA REYNOLDS *Master Crewe as Henry VIII* c.1775
(detail, see p.45)

JOSHUA REYNOLDS

Master Crewe as Henry VIII c.1775

In the eighteenth century a popular rhetorical device in portrait painting was to dress sitters in costumes representing mythological or historical figures. Outfits, props and recognisable gestures were used to highlight an aspect of the sitter's character or act as an in-joke for viewers. Famed portrait painter and one of the founders of the Royal Academy of Arts, Reynolds depicts diminutive three-year-old John Crewe as the gargantuan King Henry VIII (1491–1547), complete with spaniel puppies, who perhaps represent Henry's most favoured dogs, Cut and Ball.

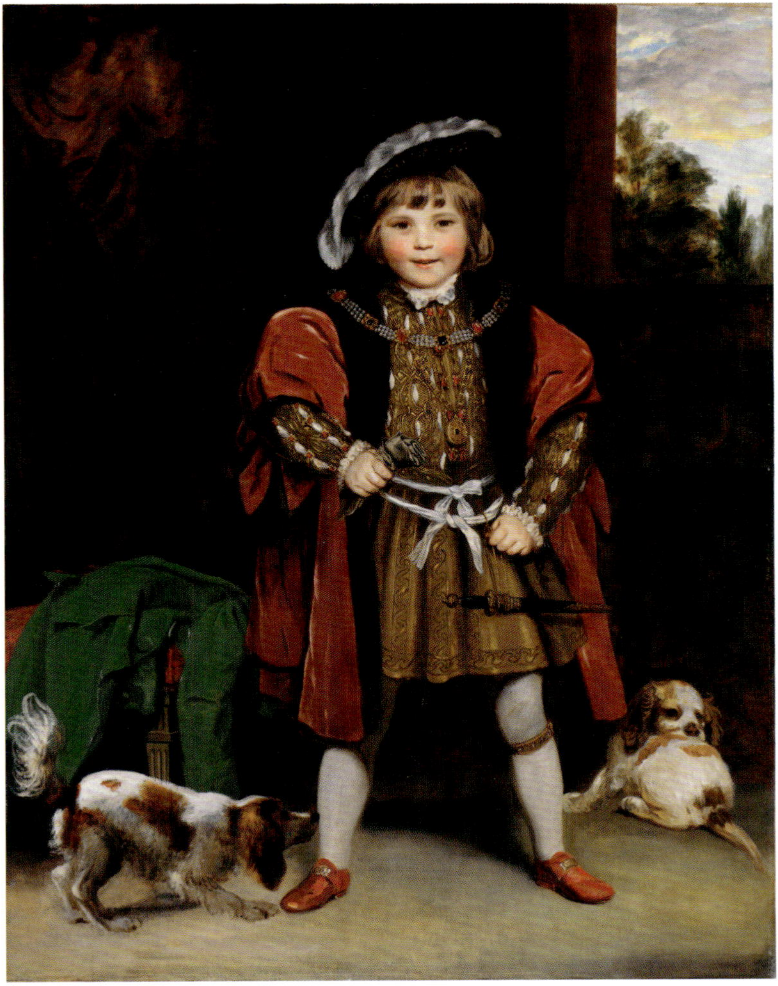

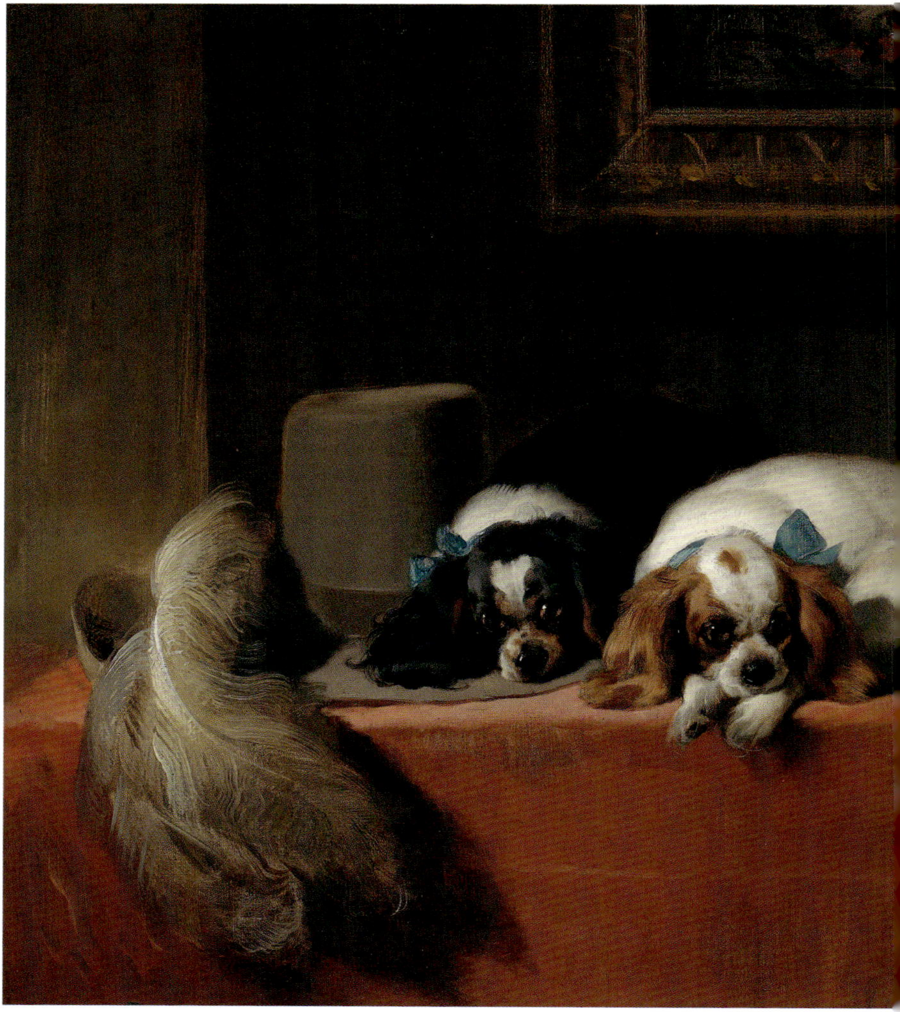

EDWIN HENRY LANDSEER

King Charles Spaniels ('The Cavalier's Pets') 1845

King Charles II (1630–85), whom these dogs are named after, reputedly issued a special decree granting the dogs access to the Houses of Parliament. True or not, these spaniels appear properly indulged and pampered. It seems butter wouldn't melt in the mouths of these two doe-eyed pups, and they certainly contribute to the 'cavalier' stereotype in this portrait of an absent Royalist – bright ribbons, long silky hair and, of course, the plumed hat.

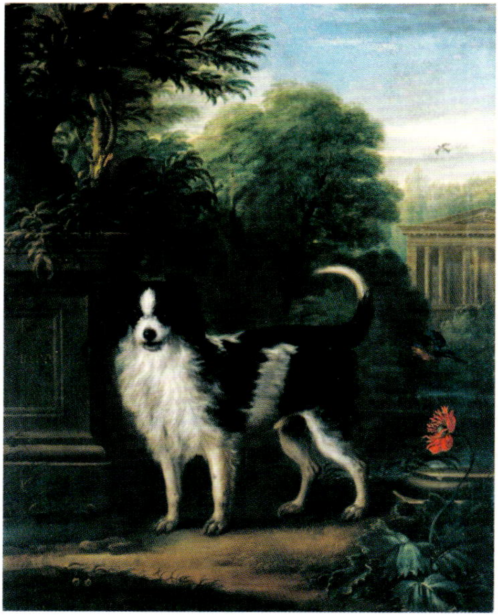

JOHN WOOTTON

Muff, a Black and White Dog c.1740–50

The history of this painting is uncertain, but it is likely the dog was called either Muff or Minx, and belonged to the Duchess of Portland, Margaret Cavendish (1715–85). This may be a memorial portrait, as the fluffy-chested dog has been afforded some symbolic flourishes befitting of nobility: a plinth with its name engraved, a fringed oriental poppy in the foreground and a swooping kingfisher – the halcyon – behind. All imply that this puppy has passed away and the painting is a loving tribute to happy memories shared.

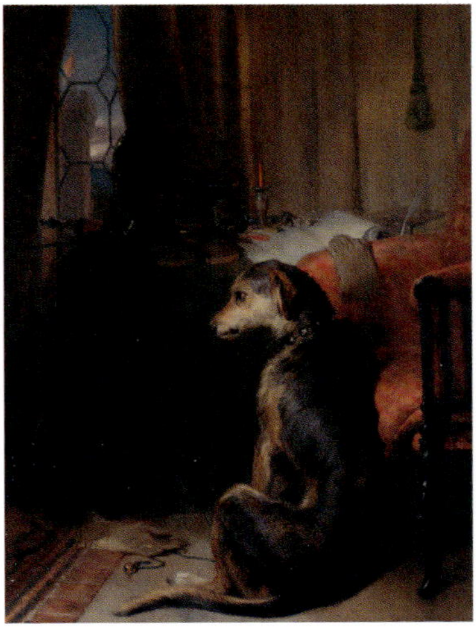

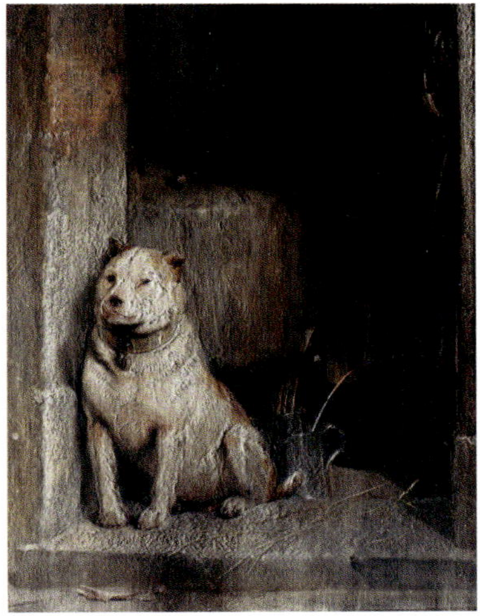

EDWIN HENRY LANDSEER

High Life 1829
Low Life 1829

Landseer uses dogs in these paintings, intended to be viewed as a pair, to convey the contrast in character and social classes of their owners. The deerhound represents an imagined aristocratic world, one a knight might have enjoyed. His tokens of chivalry lie scattered around the room – hawking gloves, rapiers, helmet, books and his quill all imply the inherent nobility of their owner. In comparison, the scarred but loyal terrier, guards the entrance to his master's butcher's shop. Here there are symbols of a tradesman surrounded by his tools, representing the hardiness of English workmen.

FRANCIS WHEATLEY

Man with a Dog c.1775

The breed of this dog is unknown, although it is likely to be a German spitz, with its telltale 'smile' and downy white tail. One of the most fashionable breeds in the late eighteenth century, the small size and general fluffiness of these dogs made them the perfect cuddly companion. They pop up in numerous paintings of the upper classes as status symbols. Thomas Gainsborough (1727–88) included a spitz in his famous painting *Mr and Mrs Hallet ('The Morning Walk')* 1785, and both that painting and this offer an arcadian ideal with dogs and humans set in pastoral landscapes.

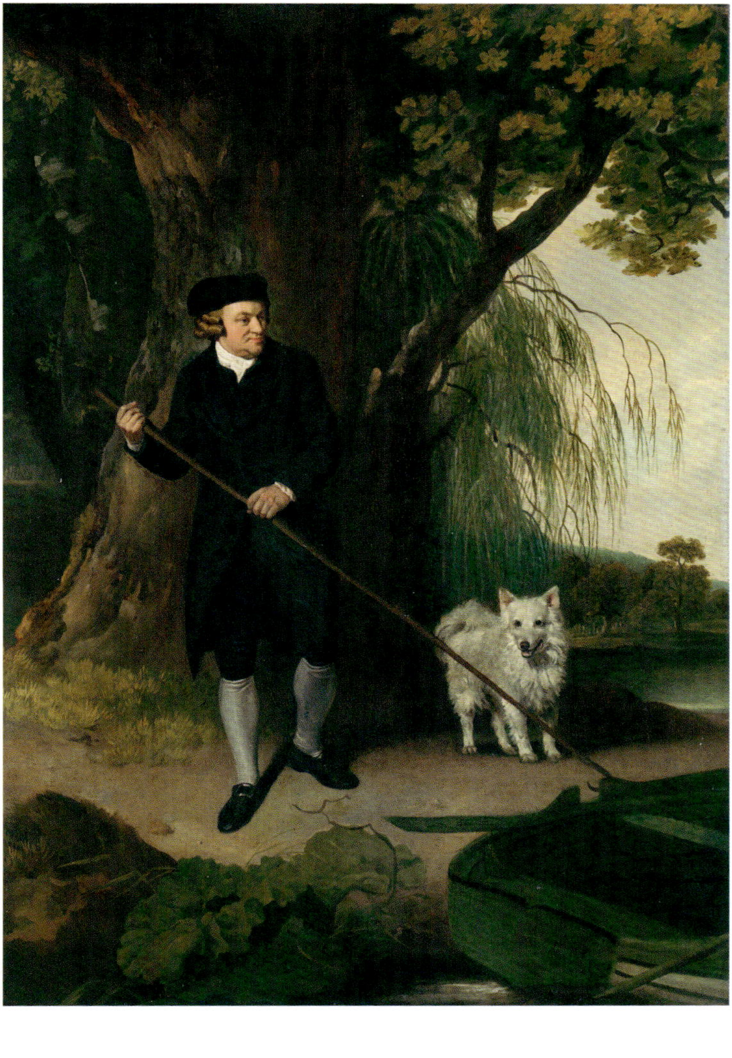

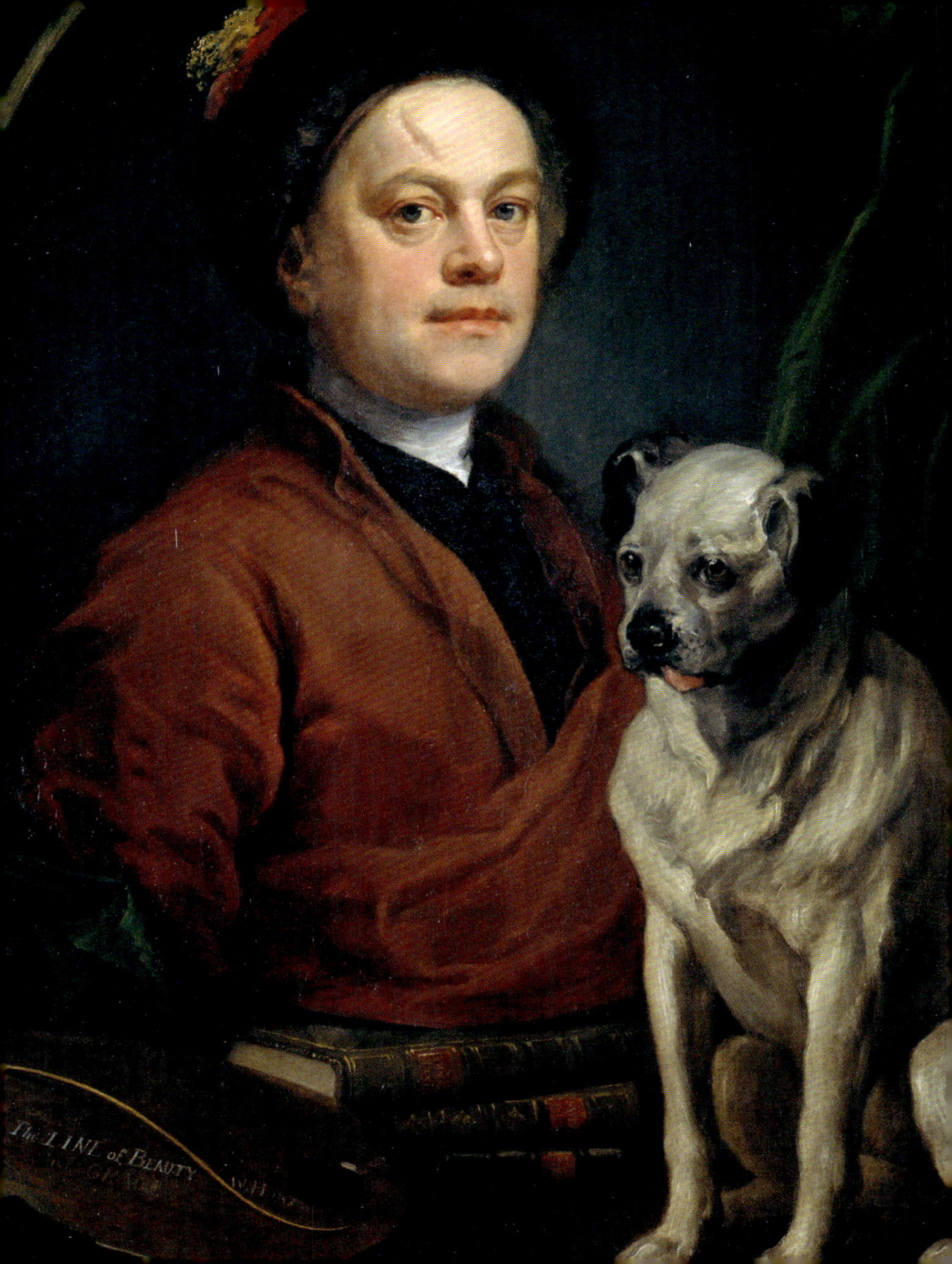
The LINE of BEAUTY

Artist's Best Friend

'These two dear little creatures are my friends. They are intelligent, loving, comical and often bored,' said David Hockney (b.1937) of his two dachshunds, Stanley and Boodgie, of whom he made forty-eight paintings and drawings. Dachshunds (or sausage dogs) it seems are a firm favourite for artists – Pablo Picasso (1881–1973) had the lovely Lump, Andy Warhol (1928–87) adored Archie, and Pierre Bonnard (1867–1947) had six sausages, each called Poucette (French for Thumberlina). Dogs make portable, fashionable and pleasing friends for artists. They perform as both muse and faithful companion during long hours in the studio, whether it's Lucian Freud (1922–2011) with his whippets, Pluto and Eli; Georgia O'Keeffe's (1887–1986) many chow chows, or Frida Kahlo's (1907–54) hairless Mexican dog, Señor Xolotl.

Throughout this chapter are works illustrating how artists have utilised their dogs – as modes of expression, to make social commentary (see opposite and p.60), to reveal their emotions (see pp.55 and 59), and as acts of devotion (see p.61).

WILLIAM HOGARTH ***The Painter and his Pug*** 1745
(detail, see p.60)

JOSEPH BARD

Photograph of Eileen Agar lying on a pebble beach at West Bay with her dog, Dandy 1934

There are nineteen personal photographs of Dandy in the Tate archive, which provide snapshots of his life with his parents, surrealist artist Eileen Agar (1899–1991) and writer Joseph Bard (1882–1975). There is Dandy sitting in the studio; Dandy taking a walk in Bath, western England; Dandy on the beach; Dandy wrestling a giant stick out of Bard's hand; Dandy reclining on a zebra rug, or Dandy investigating some swans at the Serpentine in Hyde Park, London. The collection clearly illustrates the importance of Dandy to their lives and their relationship.

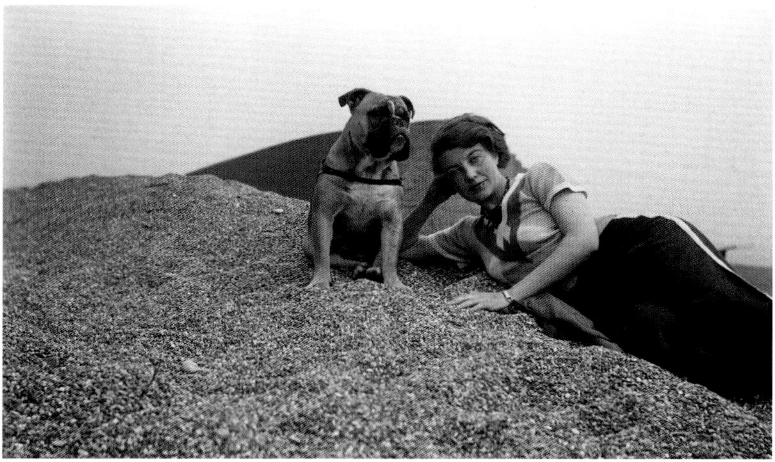

ROGER HILTON

Two Dogs 1973

St Ives artist Hilton painted this towards the end of his life, when years of alcoholism led to peripheral neuropathy leaving him unable to walk and largely confined to his bed. His later paintings become increasingly vibrant and chaotic, and the energy from the abstract dogs here is tangible, as they leap across the canvas at odd angles. Perhaps through the dynamism of these dogs, Hilton was able to access personal freedom that his life was then lacking.

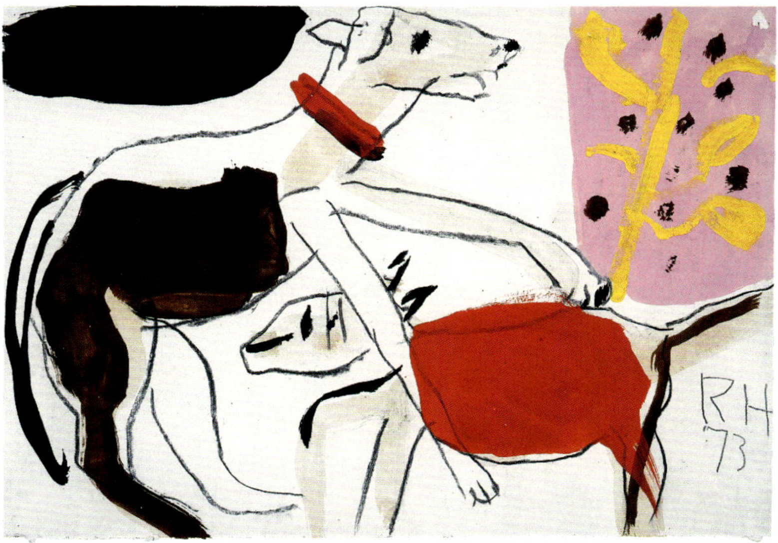

ROGER BALLEN

Puppy between Feet 1999

Supported through a pair of gnarled and filthy feet, as though emerging from a birth canal, is a newborn puppy – so fresh it can't even open its eyes, with a tiny paw, barely the size of a fingernail. The juxtaposition of the helpless and pure pup between such feet makes us wonder who the offending appendages belong to. Ballen described how it was his sitter's own idea to place the puppy between his feet, a man who would normally have ten to fifteen dogs around his house in South Africa, where this photograph was taken.

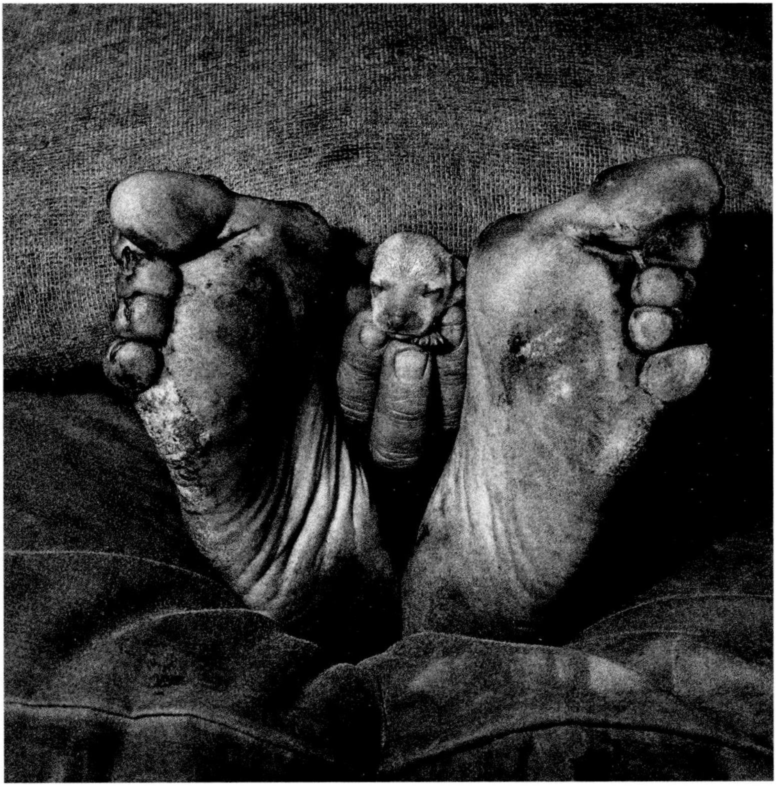

KARL WESCHKE

Feeding Dog 1976–7

Weschke's own dog, Dankoff, was the model for this painting on the cliff near the artist's house at Cape Cornwall in the west of England. Dankoff, a borzoi or Russian wolfhound, whose exceptionally long legs are particular to the breed, provides the only vertical lines in an otherwise barren, horizontal landscape. Weschke, a German prisoner-of-war, often used landscapes and his dog to explore ideas of isolation and struggle. No doubt having Dankoff as a companion was important to Weschke, as Germans living in the UK were considered to be 'aliens' for a long time after the war.

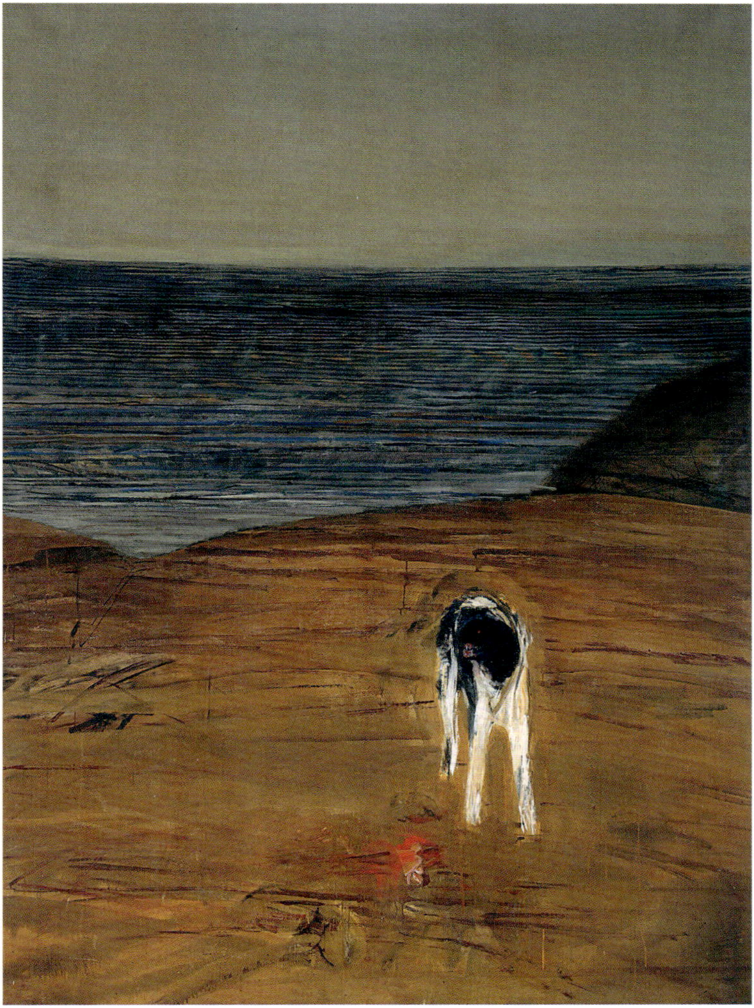

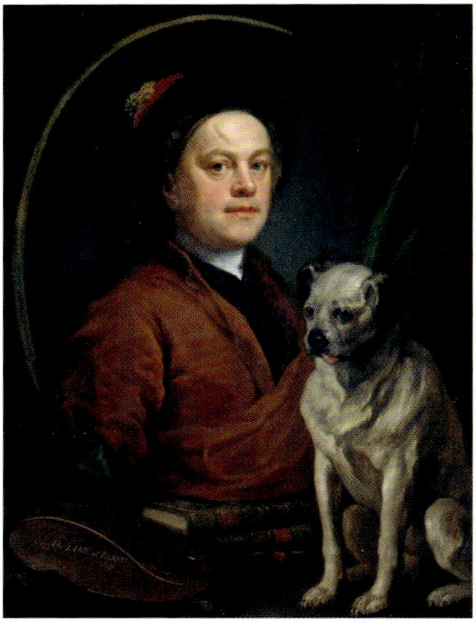

WILLIAM HOGARTH

The Painter and his Pug 1745

Trump: slack jowls, pale tufts of thinning hair, aged face with lolling tongue ... and much-loved pug of one of England's most revered artists, William Hogarth. Hogarth was a painter, printmaker, social critic and satirist, so his own self-portrait here is laden with symbolic meaning and social commentary. His beloved Trump represents his own pugnacious character, and is positioned alongside volumes of Shakespeare and Milton – marking his dog as one of the most important facets of his life. Trump also appears in other satirical paintings as an allegorical representation of his master.

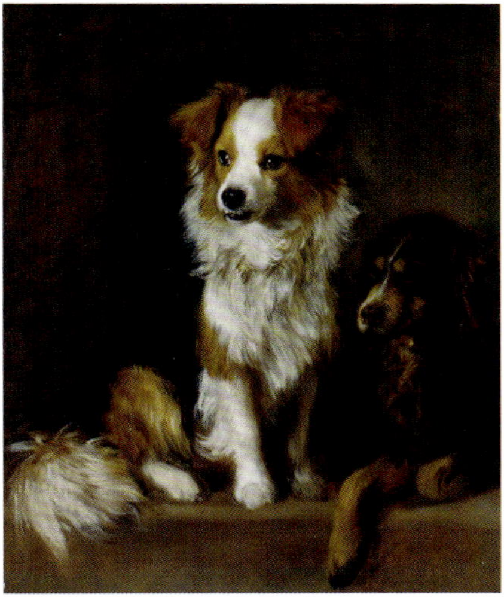

THOMAS GAINSBOROUGH

Tristram and Fox 1775–85

Despite being famed for his portraits of socialites, Gainsborough wrote to his friend saying 'I'm sick of Portraits and wish very much to take my Viol da Gamba and walk off to some sweet Village, where I can paint Landskips and enjoy the fag End of life in quietness and ease.' At heart Gainsborough was a true countryman. He loved dogs, which were included in several of his paintings, some of which were dog portraits commissioned by their owners. Here he has affectionately painted his own pets, portraying them with warmth and an understanding of their character.

KEITH ARNATT

Walking the Dog 1976–9

This pup looks like it's had a blow-dry. With splayed legs, and a direct stare into the camera lens, it seems that his little face is centred in the middle of a cotton wool ball. This photograph is from a series that Arnatt took of dogs and their owners. Getting the dogs to look directly at the camera proved to be a challenge, so Arnatt devised a plan to call out the dog's name just as he hit the release button, enabling him to capture their immediate reaction.

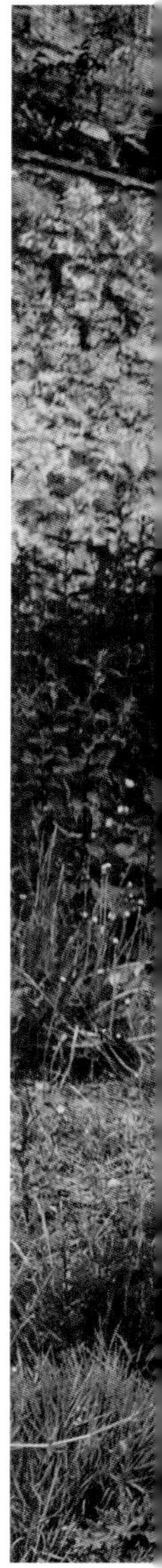

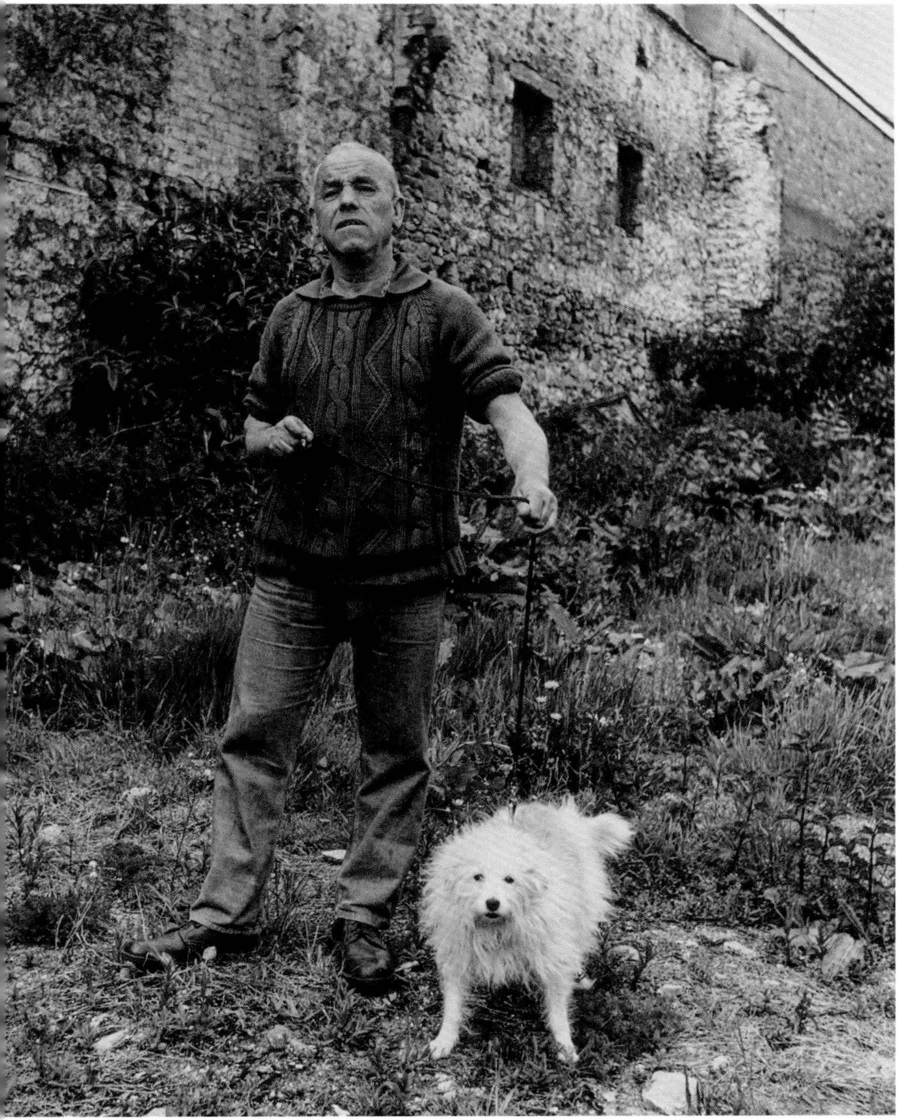

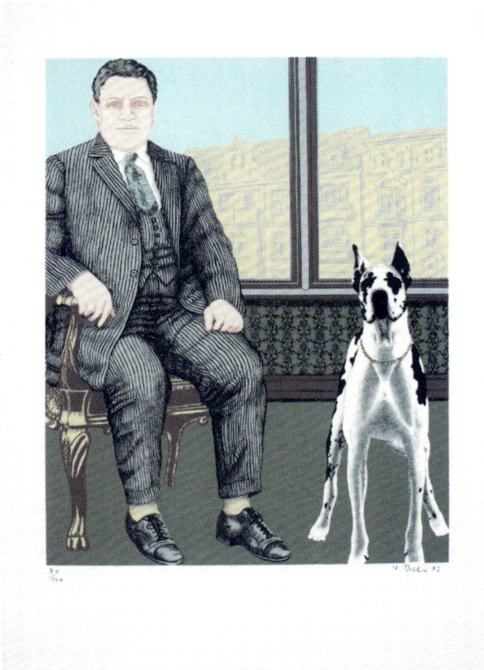

HARALD BECKER

Man and Dog 1973

The epitome of a big dog hot-shot, this large dog, possibly a piebald Great Dane, complete with gold chain, is the canine version of his human owner in a pinstripe suit. This image is part of a long tradition of portraiture with pets affirming ideas of power and masculinity. A loyal dog can make a man feel like a boss.

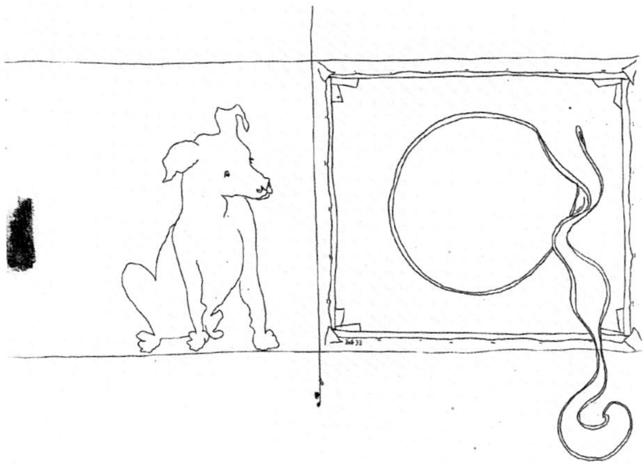

BARRY FLANAGAN

His Master's Voice 1973

The original dog for this image, Nipper, was so named because of his disposition for nipping people's legs. Famously, following the death of Nipper's owner, Mark Henry Barraud, his brother Francis was playing a voice recording of the deceased and Nipper curiously stuck his head inside the phonograph, searching for 'his master's voice'. Francis Barroud painted the scene around 1898, and eventually it became the logo we all now recognise as that of HMV, the UK music retailer. Unlike the original oil painting, Flanagan's interpretation is a rather scratchy but charming and personal etching.

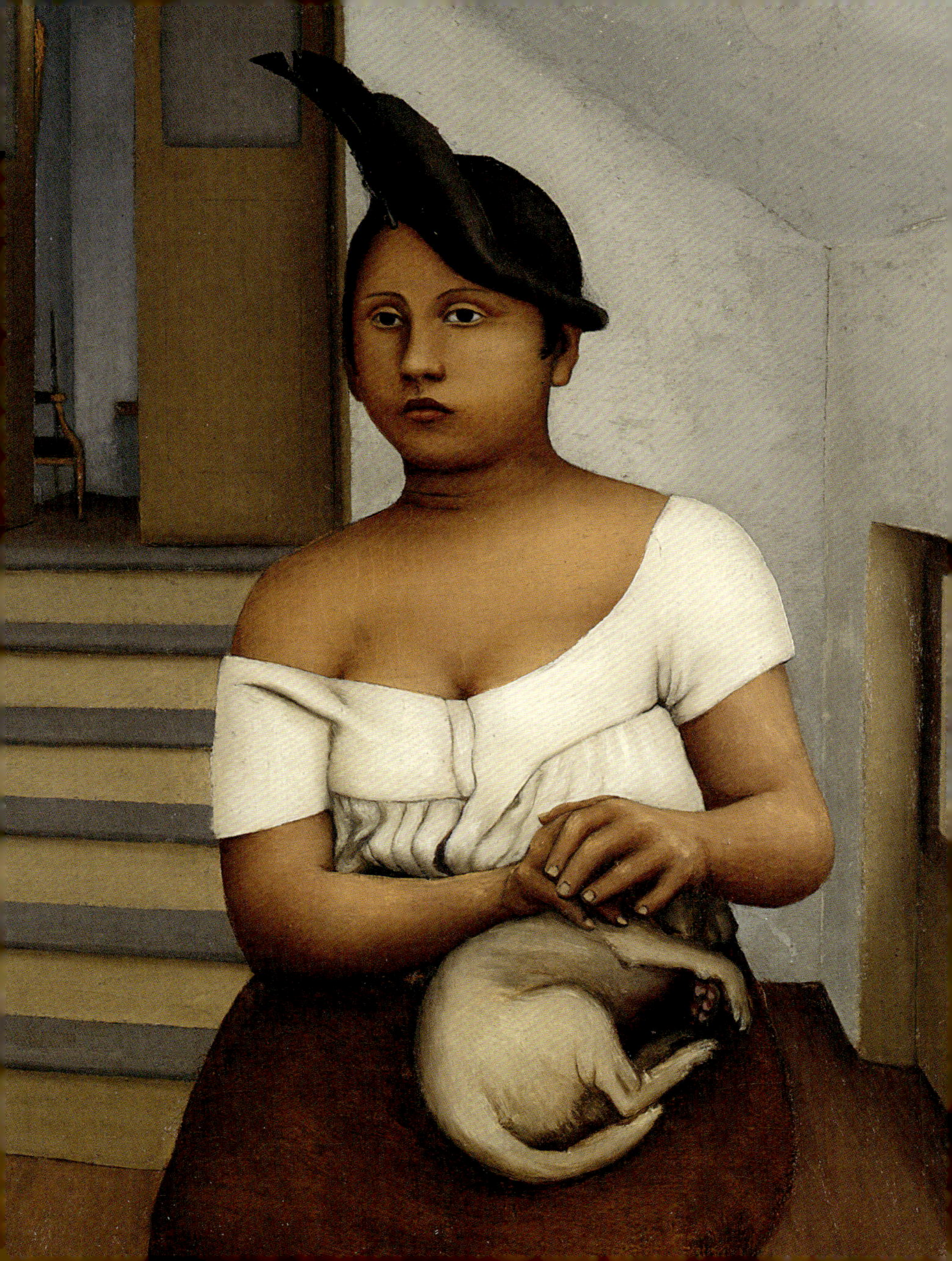

Lapdogs of Leisure

Small, warm, gentle and fluffy ... and they sit on your lap and adore you. It is no wonder that lapdogs, or 'comforters' as they were known in the sixteenth century, were exceedingly popular among the wealthy, and predominantly gentlewomen. The term 'comforter' was originally used to refer to toy spaniels, although the term 'lapdog' expanded to cover all types of small, lap-sized dogs including pug, papillon, Pekingese, shih-tzu, spitz and Maltese. In *The Canterbury Tales* (1392), Geoffrey Chaucer (1343–1400) recounts the story of a wealthy nun, or prioress who, despite her austere occupation, enjoyed the finer things in life, including her lapdogs, indicating that they were popular in the medieval period among the wealthy. Many breeds appear in later European paintings next to grand ladies and lords from the sixteenth to the eighteenth century (see p.73). Ultimately symbols of leisure, and therefore symbols of wealth, petite dogs remained steadfastly present in art until gradually they gave way to other larger canine companions in the twentieth century. The fashion for different breeds changes over time, but paintings of lapdogs remain aspirational to this day. Who wouldn't want a life of leisure with a dog on their lap?

MERAUD GUEVARA *Seated Woman with Small Dog* c.1939
(detail, p.77)

JOSHUA REYNOLDS

The Hon. Miss Monckton 1777–8

Educated and intellectual, 'blue stocking' socialite Mary Monckton's coy pose is just one alluring detail of the eighteenth-century dating profile this painting is set up to be. On trend, wearing a pale blue 'Turkish'-embroidered scarf, and sitting not just in the countryside but in the grounds of a landed estate, her depiction shows her rank and social standing. The toy spaniel was a fashionable accessory for any gentlewoman and would have signified her fidelity – to the right suitor, of course.

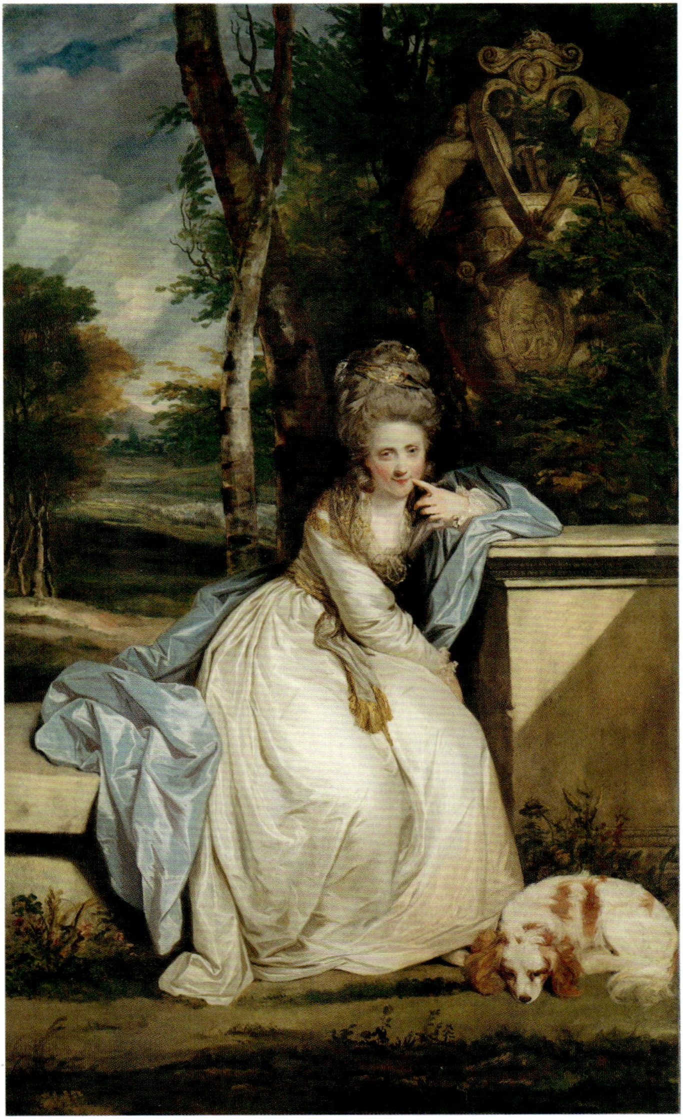

LUCIAN FREUD

Girl with a White Dog 1950–1

Freud's portraits always seem deeply personal but are frustratingly cold. We are given access to intimate situations and yet they feel uncomfortable. In this painting, Freud's first wife, Kathleen, is pregnant; her dog, who with an air of nonchalance looks outwards, beyond Freud, is only concerned with cuddling up to her. Freud was a dog lover; most famous are his beloved whippets. It was perhaps his love for canines that allowed him to capture their personalities in such fastidious detail. This bull terrier for one is quite obviously a big softie.

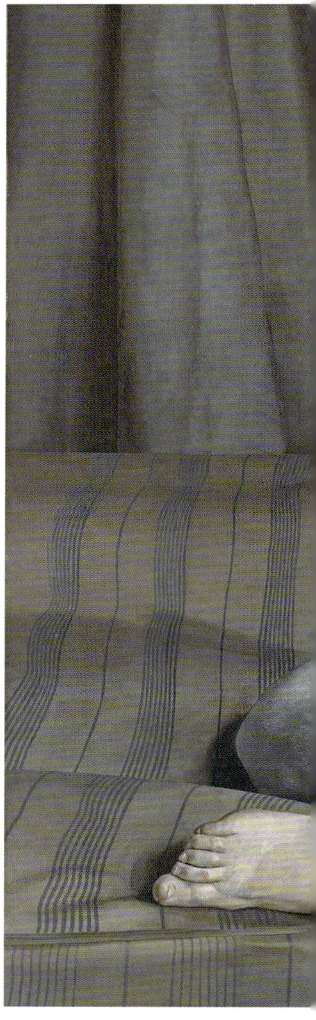

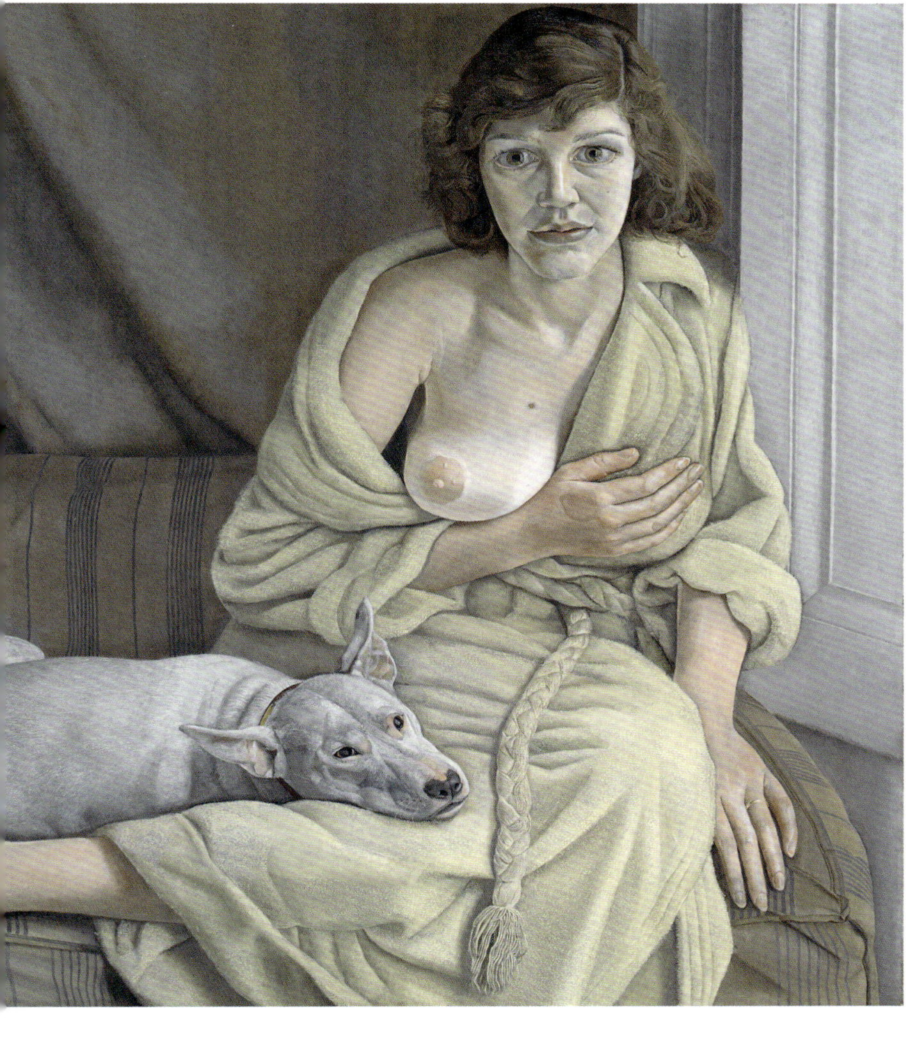

PETER LELY

Portrait of an Unknown Woman c.1670–5

There is a lot of conjecture as to who this raven-haired, bare-breasted beauty is. The exposed nipple is not typical of Lely and suggests she was a mistress. Her loyalty to the Stuarts, specifically King Charles II (1630–85), is ascertained through the spaniel she is trying to settle. If the dog is a symbol for the sovereign, then it could be assumed that she has a powerful connection to the king himself, since the spaniel is looking up adoringly at her, begging for attention.

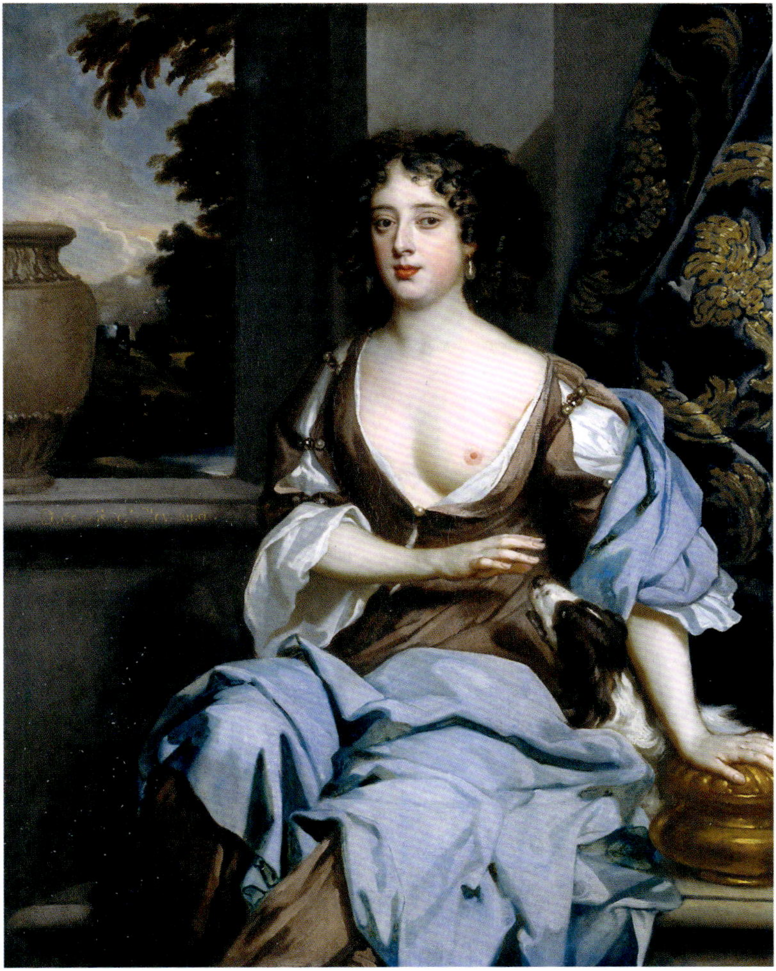

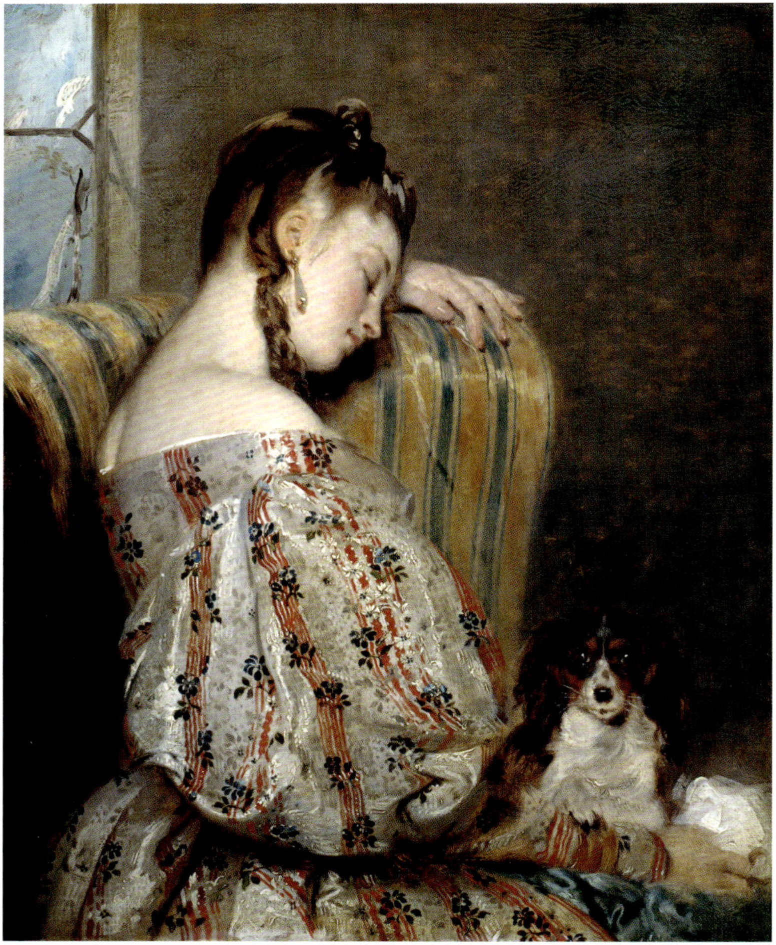

HENRY WYATT

Vigilance 1835

Humans don't deserve dogs. We all know that. Here one tiny protective paw rests on his mistress's hand as he watches on, suspicious of the painter, tenacious and vigilant in his task of lapdog security. Wyatt was a popular portraitist in the nineteenth century, and although he has spent considerable time on the beautiful fabrics of this woman's dress and the shine in her hair, it is her faithful lapdog who takes centre stage in this painting.

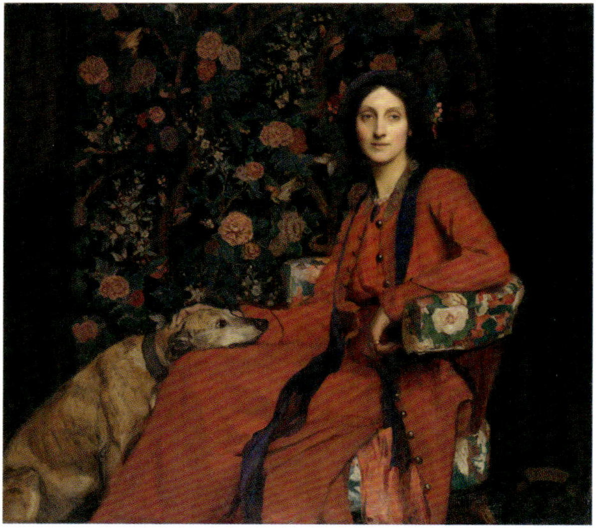

GEORGE SPENCER WATSON

Hilda and Maggie 1911

Is there any animal that can convey love in such an honest way as a dog? Completely enraptured by Hilda (dancer, mime artist and wife to Watson), Maggie the dog is resigned to resting her head dotingly on her lap. The intimate bond between dog and human in this painting is palpable. The feelings were obviously mutual, as Watson painted Maggie into many other family portraits, including one titled *Four Loves I Found, A Woman, A Child, A Horse and A Hound* 1922, which features Hilda, their daughter Mary on a pet horse, and Maggie trotting faithfully alongside, tongue merrily lolling.

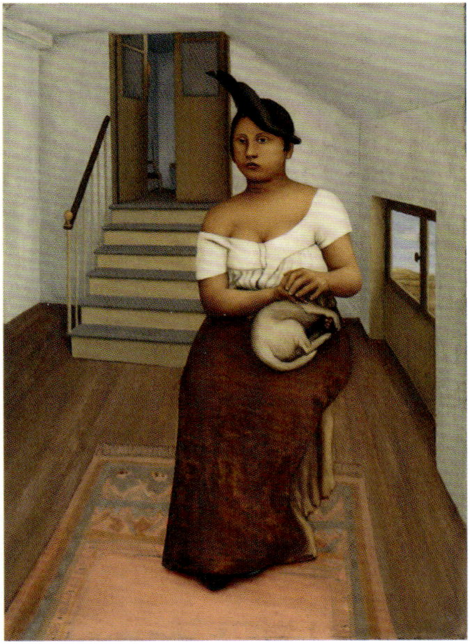

MERAUD GUEVARA

Seated Woman with Small Dog c.1939

Born into the Guinness family, Guevara was a wealthy heiress, yet had little interest in their stout fortunes and instead set upon a life of painting. In this work the trope of a lady with her lapdog is subverted; the sitter is not a coquettish object to be possessed but a solid, statuesque entity that the room around her can barely contain. The uncanny perspective of the room shrinks the walls around her as her hands imitate the effect over her dog.

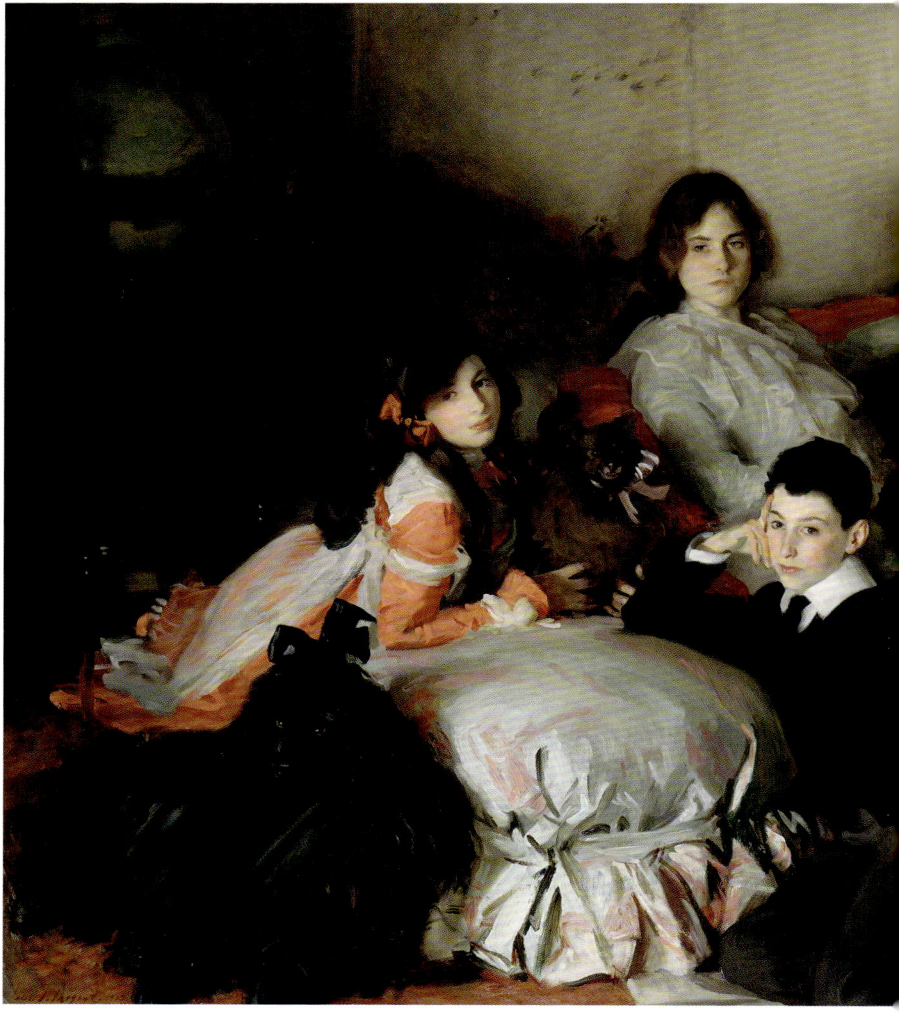

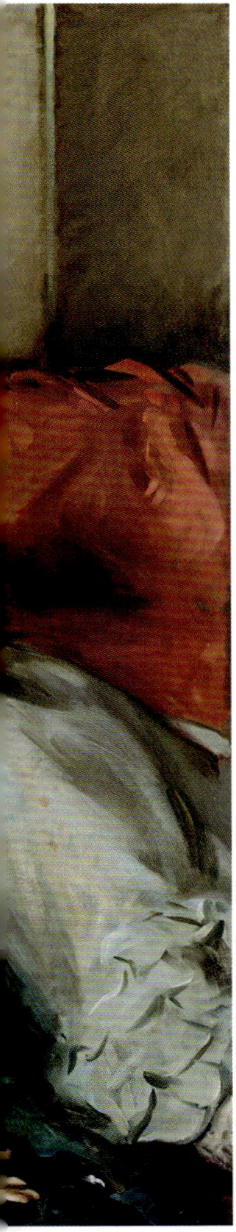

JOHN SINGER SARGENT

Essie, Ruby and Ferdinand, Children of Asher Wertheimer 1902

Wealthy children from the Wertheimer family sit with their dogs; both humans and animals, as *The Spectator* noted, 'bedecked with bows, and the air we feel smells of scent and burnt pastilles'. With the globe in the background, ottoman and rich fabrics, this is a typical scene of comfortable, cultured wealth. Sargent was friends with the family and carried out his largest private commission for them – twelve portraits in total. Dogs here are playmates for bored children, and the poodle in the foreground, Noble, affirms their social standing.

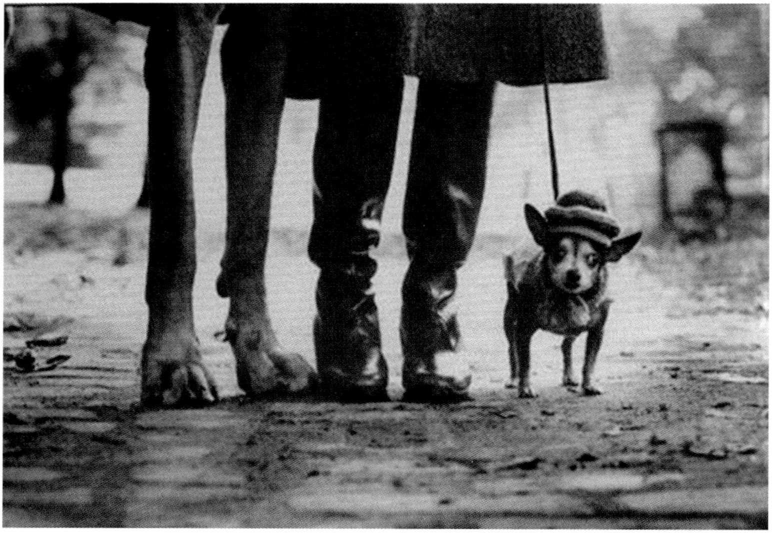

ELLIOT ERWITT

New York City 1974, printed later

Erwitt, a member of Magnum Photos, an international photographic cooperative, did not set out to capture dogs on film and yet now they are part of some of his most famous works, with several publications based solely on their reproduction. He has described how, beyond their easy charm, his photographs of dogs seem to have allegorical meaning to humans and portray something about the human condition: 'I don't know of any other animals closer to us in qualities of heart, sentiment and loyalty'. Presumably the pair of long legs on the left belong to a Great Dane.

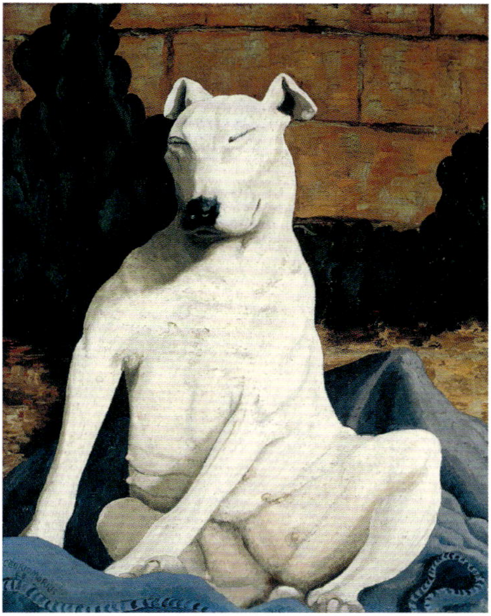

CEDRIC MORRIS

Belle of Bloomsbury 1948

Swirl, or 'Swirlie' as she is referred to in a faded photo album in the Tate archive, is the magnificent star of this portrait. Painted fourteen years after her death as a gift from the artist to his sister Nancy, Swirl was the beautiful bull terrier in residence with the Bloomsbury Group. Swirl would have been privy to the wild parties for sapphic socialites that Nancy threw for her friends and lovers, but here she is taking some much needed time out from the festivities.

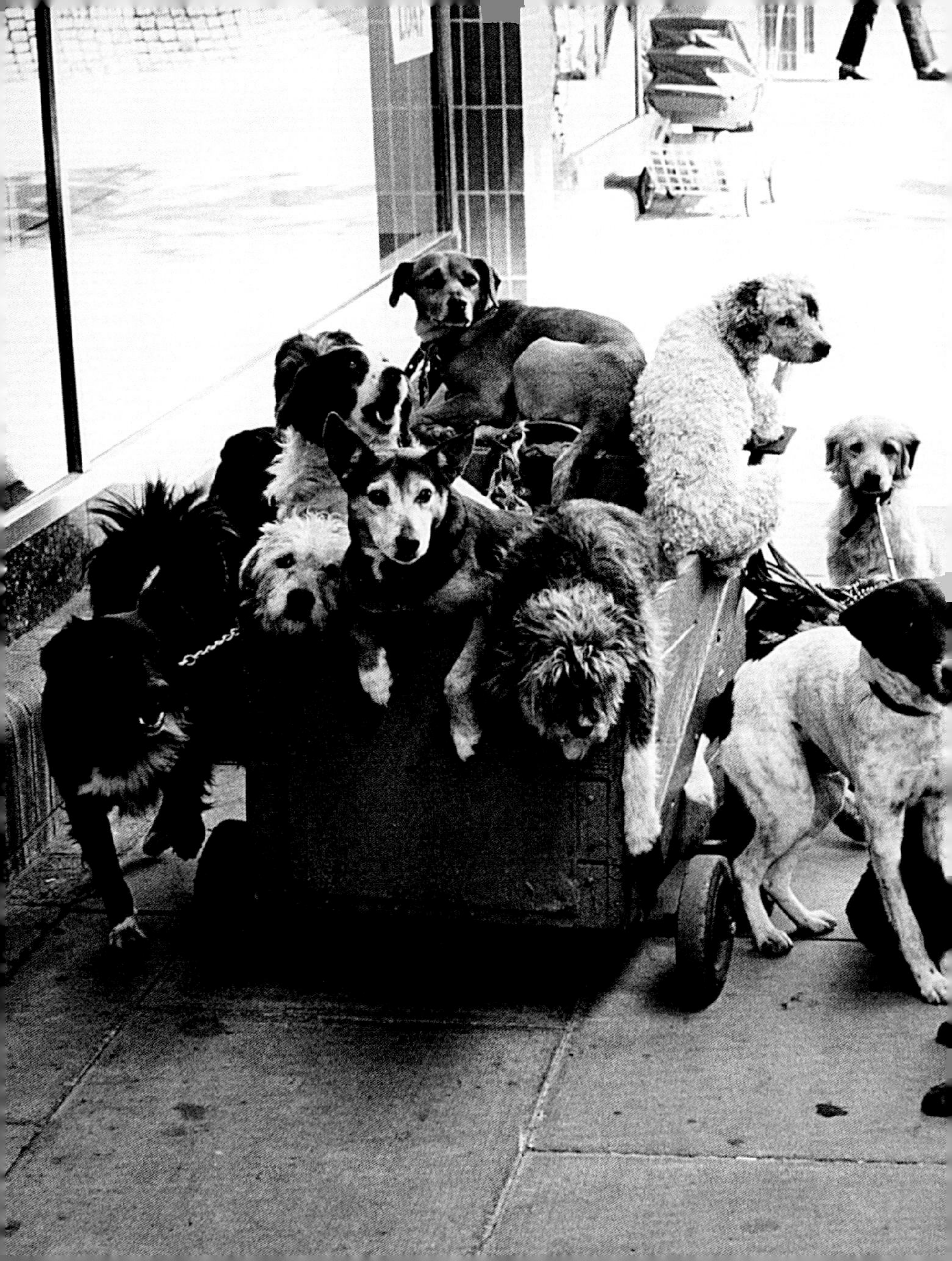

Creating Fido

In Latin the word *fido* relates to trust, so it is really no surprise that it is also the generic term we use for a pet dog. Humans rely on dogs. We have created a loving and co-dependent relationship with them, and to extricate them from our lives after thousands of years of symbiotic companionship would be near-impossible.

The dog as a concept inspires artists. Dogs allow artistic expression – they simultaneously give us licence to be sentimental while also connecting to something deeply primal and animalistic. In art dogs can represent a great many things: they can act as a tool for communication, or as a metaphor. Their presence can be profound, or might be purely a straightforward reflection of a domestic scene. Sometimes they represent indulgent acts of devotion to a dear pet and friend; sometimes the dog is just one facet of a theatrical artistic persona. The simple, good-natured character of a dog can be subverted and made uncanny, used to catch the viewer off-guard (p.88), or it can be used cynically or humorously (p.86). Ultimately dogs in their many forms and guises in art reflect how we view the world and our relationships, whether that is exploitative, or selfless and generous.

ELLIOT ERWITT *London* 1974, printed later
(detail, see p.93)

BRITON RIVIÈRE

Sympathy c.1878

This little girl is sitting on what is perhaps the naughty step, or maybe she has been excluded from adult company, while her loyal fido remains beside her offering some camaraderie. Rivière became immensely popular in the Victorian period for such sentimental works, yet the compassion of a dog transcends time and is something we still find ourselves obsessing over today, even if now it is more likely to be through puppy videos on Instagram. Fundamentally humans are all sentimental fools when it comes to dogs.

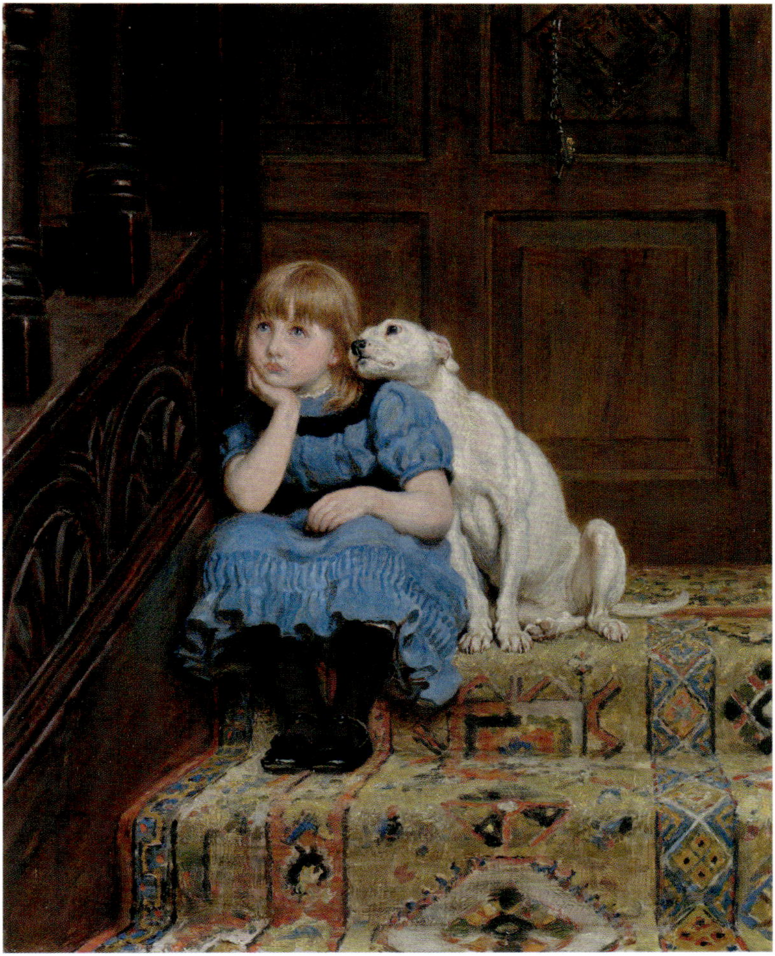

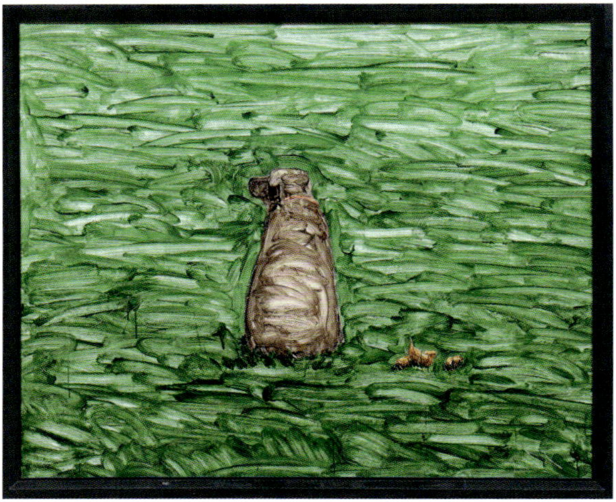

NEIL JENNEY

Dog and Shit 1970

In 1978, the art critic Marcia Tucker put on an exhibition entitled *Bad Paintings* where she showed independent realists, including Neil Jenney. Embracing the term 'bad', Jenney told a friend 'it would be better to have a good idea and do it terrible! So then I started the "Bad Paintings" which seemed like a new realism to people'. He rejected the decorative and expressive qualities of modern abstract art and instead aimed for a modern expression of classical realism, often incorporating the sculptural nature of the frame itself in his work. There is a sense of dry humour in this piece; a dog waits patiently next to its own excrement as Jenney challenges us on what makes a good or bad painting.

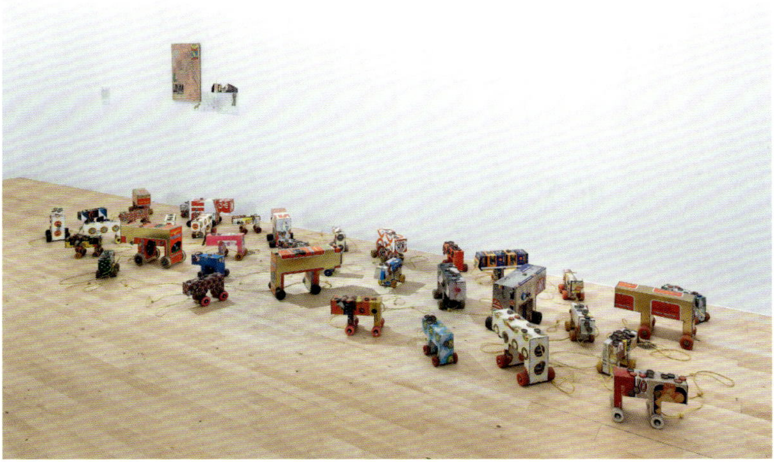

FRANCIS ALŸS

Collectors 2006

These thirty-six tin dogs invite comparison with the robotic dog K9 from the British science-fiction television series, *Doctor Who*. Their brightly-coloured toy-like construction of magnets, tin containers, nylon, wood and photographs is seemingly haphazard. The title of the installation alludes to Alÿs's earliest work, a performance piece where the artist walked through the streets of Mexico City pulling a small toy dog, whose magnetic body picked up various metal detritus from the streets, 'collecting' souvenirs from its journey. The collection of dogs invites stories and connections between location, space and memory.

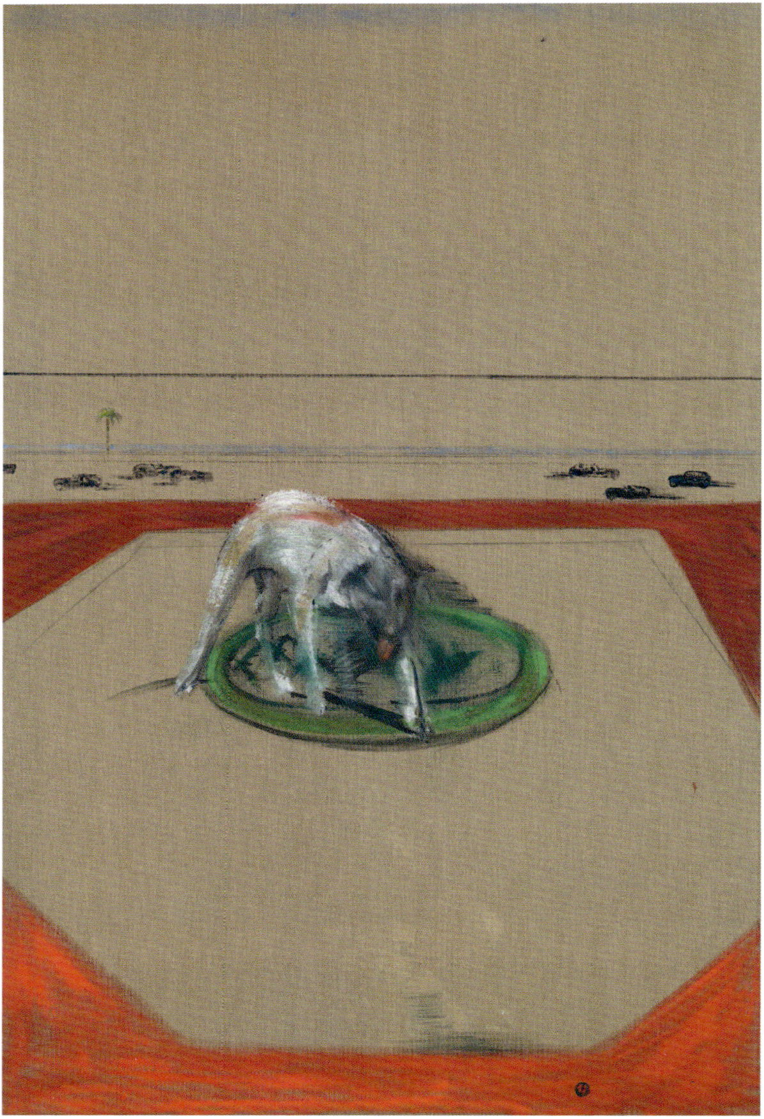

FRANCIS BACON

Dog 1952

Dragged paint across the canvas gives a blurred effect to this dog spiralling out of control. The hanging tongue and green circle present an impression that the dog is in an endless spin, perhaps chasing its tail or some unseen creature in a psychotic perpetual chase. As a starting point for this painting, Bacon used Eadweard Muybridge's *Animal Locomotion* 1884–7 – a series of animals and humans photographed in sequences to reveal aspects of motion and movement. Bacon's result is a raw and painful image, the dog perhaps a metaphor for our own frantic race through life.

PETER DOIG

Double Dog 2012

Scottish-born painter Doig has created a light-hearted etching depicting a ‘Scottie’ and a ‘Westie’, both breeds native to his country of birth. Doig’s etching is no doubt inspired by the branding on James Buchanan’s Scotch whisky brand – Black & White – which features the same pair. Buchanan, a ‘whisky baron’ of the nineteenth century, was said to have designed the label himself after being inspired at a dog show. Scottish terriers enjoy public favour still, thanks to Queen Victoria’s tastes, and appear in everything from game pieces in Monopoly, to boxes of shortbread adorned in tartan.

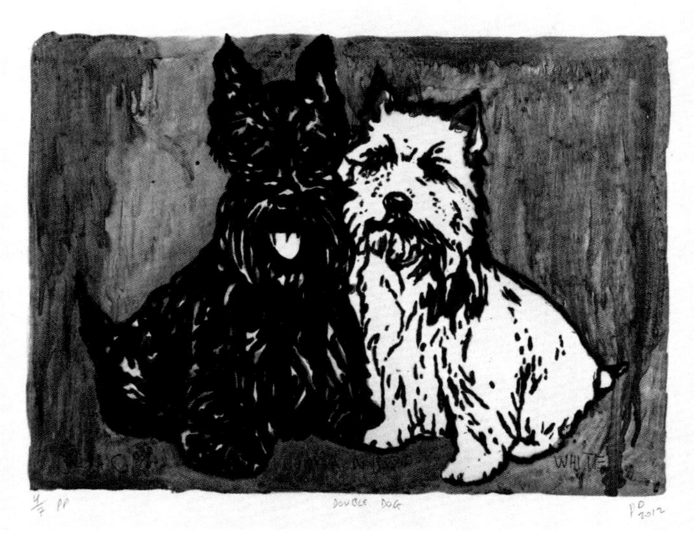

CRAIGIE AITCHISON

Model and Dog 1974–5

Recumbent naked women with dogs was a theme employed by Renaissance painter Titian (1488–1576), an artist whom Aitchison greatly admired. In Titian's *Venus of Urbino* 1538, a tiny dog lies at its mistress's feet, a symbol of fidelity. Such European nudes are traditionally seductive, intended for the sexual pleasure of the viewer. Typically the expression of the nude acted as an invitation, while symbolic allegories around them affirmed their submissiveness, fidelity or wealth. It is the white dog rather than the woman here that holds the viewer's gaze, with one single perfectly round dot of an eye. This dog is presumably one of the artist's own Bedlington terriers, which appear in many of his other works.

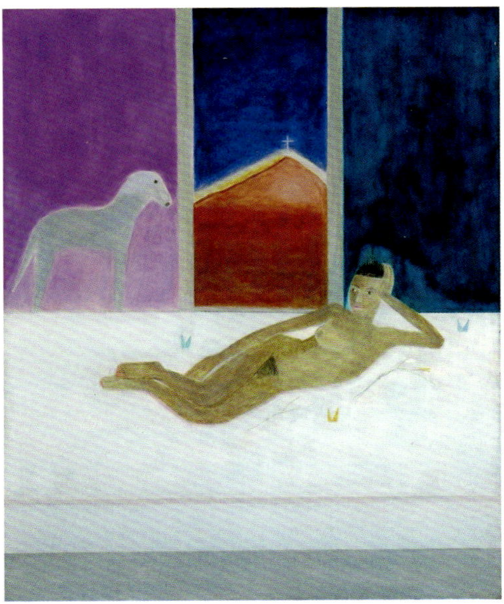

HENRI GAUDIER-BRZESKA

A Dog c.1913

Gaudier-Brzeska died young, at just twenty-three-years-old while in the trenches, serving in the French army. Despite producing art for only four years before his death, his artistic output had great impact on avant-garde sculpture in the twentieth century. The long-limbed dog pictured here was sketched in chalk and ink, and made for a marble relief currently in the Art Institute of Chicago. Despite the sparse ink lines, this simple drawing has a sculptural depth and holds a heaviness of feeling.

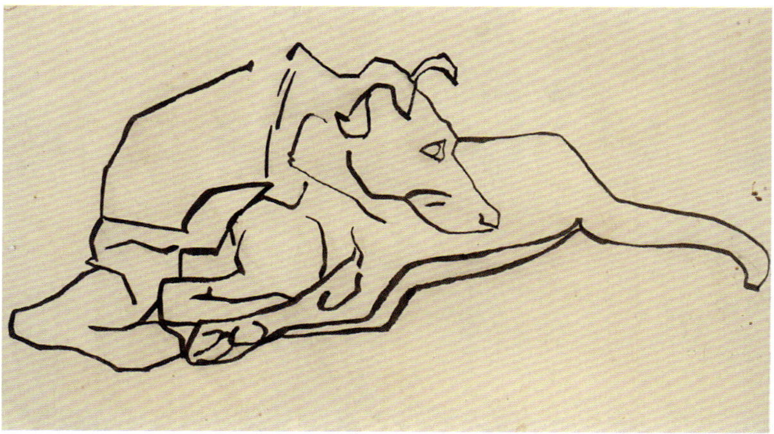

ELLIOT ERWITT

London 1974, printed later

Tumbling out of a wagon unable to contain them, is a sprawling mass of mutts, pups, pooches and good boys - all breeds, all ages and all personalities. Perhaps the owner of the cart was employed to take them on walks, or as doggy daycare. Or perhaps they, like so many of us, simply couldn't say no to their furry friends. Erwitt, too, is clearly infatuated.

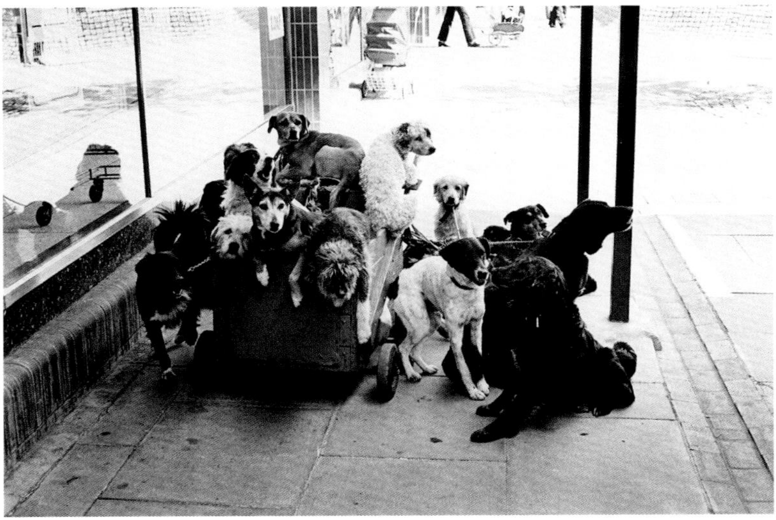

ILLUSTRATED WORKS

Measurements of artworks are given in centimetres, height before width and depth

CRAIGIE AITCHISON 1926–2009
Model and Dog 1974–5
Oil paint on canvas
221 x 188
p.91

FRANCIS ALŸS b.1959
Collectors 2006
36 tin dogs, magnets, metal, nylon strings, map mounted on wood, photographs, graphite and acrylic paint on paper
Display dimensions variable
p.87

KEITH ARNATT 1930–2008
Walking the Dog 1976–9
Gelatin silver print on paper
39 x 30.5
p.63

FRANCIS BACON 1909–92
Dog 1952
Oil paint and sand on canvas
198.1 x 137.2
p.88

ROGER BALLEN b.1950
Puppy between Feet 1999
Gelatin silver print on paper
36 x 36.2
p.57

JOSEPH BARD 1882–1975
Photograph of Eileen Agar lying on a pebble beach at West Bay with her dog, Dandy 1934
Black and white photograph
6.9 x 11.5
pp.4 (detail), 54

HARRY BATES 1850–99
Hounds in Leash 1888–9
Plaster
116 x 220 x 108
p.15

HARALD BECKER b.1940
Man and Dog 1973
Screenprint on paper
62.9 x 50.2
p.64

PETER DOIG b.1959
Double Dog 2012
Etching and aquatint on paper
22.5 x 36
p.90

ELLIOT ERWITT b.1928
London 1974, printed later
Gelatin silver print on paper
31.5 x 47.1
p.93

New York City 1974, printed later
Gelatin silver print on paper
30.5 x 40.5
p.80

BARRY FLANAGAN 1941–2009
His Master's Voice 1973
Etching on paper
20.9 x 24.5
p.65

LUCIAN FREUD 1922–2011
Girl with a White Dog 1950–1
Oil paint on canvas
76.2 x 101.6
p.71

CHARLES WELLINGTON FURSE 1868–1904
Diana of the Uplands 1903–4
Oil paint on canvas
236.9 x 179.1
pp.32 (detail), 36

THOMAS GAINSBOROUGH 1727–88
Tristram and Fox c.1775–85
Oil paint on canvas
61 x 50.8
p.61

HENRI GAUDIER-BRZESKA 1891–1915
A Dog c.1913
Ink and chalk on paper
17.8 x 31.8
p.92

MERAUD GUEVARA 1904–33
Seated Woman with Small Dog c.1939
Oil paint and graphite on canvas
89 x 65
pp.66 (detail), 77

ROGER HILTON 1911–75
Two Dogs 1973
Gouache and charcoal on paper
38 x 56
p.55

LUBAINA HIMID b.1954
Freedom and Change 1984
Wood, textiles, cardboard, paint, graphite, coloured pencil, chalk and ink
309.6 x 590 x 6
p.37

WILLIAM HOGARTH 1697–1764
The Painter and his Pug 1745
Oil paint on canvas
90 x 69.9
pp.52 (detail), 60

JACOB HUYSMANS c.1630–96
Portrait of a Lady, as Diana c.1674
Oil paint on canvas
119.7 x 101.3
p.39

NEIL JENNEY b.1945
Dog and Shit 1970
Acrylic paint on canvas
142.2 x 193
p.86

CHRIS KILLIP 1946–2020
Whippet Fancier 1973, printed 2012–13
Gelatin silver print on paper
44 x 36
p.28

EDWIN HENRY LANDSEER 1802–73
High Life 1829
Oil paint on mahogany
45.7 x 34.9
p.49

Low Life 1829
Oil paint on mahogany
45.7 x 35.2
p.49

Sleeping Bloodhound exhibited 1835
Oil paint on canvas
101.6 x 127
p.14

A Distinguished Member of the Humane Society exhibited 1838
Oil paint on canvas
111.8 x 143.5
p.20

King Charles Spaniels ('The Cavalier's Pets') 1845
Oil paint on canvas
69.8 x 90.2
p.46

Alexander and Diogenes 1848
Oil paint on canvas
112.4 x 142.9
p.35

PETER LELY 1618–80
Portrait of an Unknown Woman c.1670–5
Oil paint on canvas
125.1 x 100.3
p.73

PAUL McCARTHY b.1945
Dog 2000
Part of *Cubitt Print Box*
Colour photograph on plastic
8.6 x 18
p.34

CEDRIC MORRIS 1889–1982
Belle of Bloomsbury 1948
Oil paint on canvas
66.3 x 55.2
p.81, cover

JOHN MURPHY b.1945
Investigations of a Dog (Pictor) 1984–96
Oil paint on canvas
265 x 199
p.41

SIDNEY NOLAN 1917–92
Landscape – Miner with Dog 1973
Part of *Landscapes*
Screenprint on paper
76.2 x 76.3
p.25

EDUARDO PAOLOZZI 1924–2005
H. Left: Television Series 'Lost in Space': Robot as in 'Forbidden Planet'. Right: Soviet Dog and Man Exit from Space Chamber 1971
Part of *Cloud Atomic Laboratory*
Etching on paper
27 x 38.1
p.31

PAULA REGO b.1935
Doctor Dog 1982
Lithograph on paper
71 x 105.3
p.22

JOSHUA REYNOLDS 1723–92
Master Crewe as Henry VIII c.1775
Oil paint on canvas
139 x 111
pp.42 (detail), 45

The Hon. Miss Monckton 1777–8
Oil paint on canvas
240 x 147.3
p.69

BRITON RIVIÈRE 1840–1920
Sympathy c.1878
Oil paint on canvas
45.1 x 37.5
p.85

WILLIAM ROBERTS 1895–1980
Study for 'Guarding the Masterpiece' c.1964
Graphite on paper
17.8 x 12.7
p.26

JOHN SINGER SARGENT 1856–1925
Essie, Ruby and Ferdinand, Children of Asher Wertheimer 1902
Oil paint on canvas
161.3 x 193.7
p.78

JOHN NOST SARTORIUS 1759–1828
The Earl of Darlington Fox-Hunting with the Raby Pack: Going to Cover 1805
Oil paint on canvas
71.4 x 91.4
p.13

COLIN SELF b.1941
Guard Dog on a Missile Base, No. 1 1965
Graphite, ink, watercolour and crayon on card
55.6 x 76.2
p.30

ATTRIBUTED TO JAMES SEYMOUR c.1702–52
Pointer Bitch c.1740
Oil paint on canvas
92.1 x 114.6
p.13

GEORGE STUBBS 1724–1806
A Couple of Foxhounds 1792
Oil paint on canvas
101.6 x 127
pp.8 (detail), 16

PETER TILLEMANS 1684–1734
Foxhunting in Wooded Country c.1720–30
Oil paint on canvas
102.2 x 117.2
p.11

GEORGE SPENCER WATSON 1869–1934
Hilda and Maggie 1911
Oil paint on canvas
127 x 144.8
p.76

KARL WESCHKE 1925–2005
Feeding Dog 1976–7
Oil paint on canvas
197.7 x 152.3
p.59

FRANCIS WHEATLEY 1747–1801
Man with a Dog c.1775
Oil paint on canvas
97.8 x 73.7
p.51

THOMAS WOODWARD 1801–52
The Rat Catcher and his Dogs exhibited 1824
Oil paint on mahogany
43.2 x 54
pp.18 (detail), 23

JOHN WOOTTON 1682–1764
Muff, a Black and White Dog c.1740–50
Oil paint on canvas
125.1 x 101.6
p.48

HENRY WYATT 1794–1840
Vigilance 1835
Oil paint on canvas
34.9 x 29.8
p.74

CREDITS

COPYRIGHT
© The estate of Craigie Aitchison 91

© Francis Alÿs. Courtesy the artist and Galerie Peter Kilchmann, Zurich 87

© Keith Arnatt Estate. All rights reserved. DACS 2021 62–3

© The Estate of Francis Bacon. All rights reserved. DACS 2021 88

© Roger Ballen, courtesy Hamiltons Gallery, London 57

© Estate of Joseph Bard 4–5, 54

Harald Becker © DACS 2021 64

© Peter Doig. All Rights Reserved, DACS 2021 90

© Elliot Erwitt/Magnum Photos 80, 82, 93

© The Estate of Barry Flanagan / Bridgeman Images 65

© Estate of Meraud Guevara 66, 77

© Estate of Roger Hilton. All rights reserved, DACS 2021 55
Copyright of Lubaina Himid 37

Jenney Archive LLC 86

© Estate of Chris Killip 28

© Paul McCarthy. Courtesy the artist and Hauser & Wirth 34

© The Cedric Morris Foundation / Bridgeman Images cover, 81

Copyright John Murphy 41

© The Sidney Nolan Trust. All rights reserved, DACS 2021 25

© The Paolozzi Foundation, Licensed by DACS 2021 31

© Paula Rego 22

Estate of John David Roberts. By permission of the Treasury Solicitor 26

© Colin Self. All rights reserved, DACS 2021 30

© Tate, 2021 70–1

© The Estate of Karl Weschke. All rights reserved, DACS 2021 59

PHOTOGRAPHY
Courtesy of Roger Ballen, Hamiltons Gallery, London 57

Courtesy of the artist and Hollybush Gardens. Photo: Andy Keate 37

© Tate, 2021 cover, 4–5, 8, 13, 15, 16, 20–1, 22, 25, 26, 28, 30, 31, 32, 34, 36, 39, 38, 41, 42, 45, 46–7, 48, 49, 51, 52, 54, 55, 59, 60, 61, 62–3, 64, 65, 66, 69, 70–1, 73, 74, 76, 77, 78–9, 80, 81, 82, 85, 86, 87, 88, 91, 92, 93; /Oliver Cowling 90; /Andrew Dunkley 35; /Mark Heathcote 11, 18, 23; Seraphina Neville and Oliver Cowling 14